Binge-Watching Eats

Binge-Watching Eats

THEMED SNACKS AND DRINKS
FOR YOUR NEXT BINGE WATCH

KATHERINE BEBO

RYLAND PETERS & SMALL
LONDON • NEW YORK

Dedication

For Jonathan and Phoebe. An incentive to finally fix your TV? Happy watching and happy eating!

Designer Paul Stradling
Picture Researcher Christina Borsi
Production Controller Mai-Ling Collyer
Art Director Leslie Harrington
Editorial Director Julia Charles
Publisher Cindy Richards

Indexer Hilary Bird

First published in 2019 by
Ryland Peters & Small
20–21 Jockey's Fields
London WC1R 4BW
and
341 E 116th St
New York NY 10029

www.rylandpeters.com

10 9 8 7 6 5 4 3 2 1

Recipe collection compiled by Julia Charles. Text copyright © Bronte Aurell, Miranda Ballard, Kiki Bee, Mickael Benichou, Julia Charles, Lydia Clark, Chloe Coker, Felipe Fuentes Cruz, Julian Day, Jesse Estes, Ben Fordham, Liz Franklin, Tonia George, Victoria Glass, Nicola Graimes, Tori Haschka, Carol Hilker, Jennifer Joyce, Jackie Kearney, Dan May, Claire McDonald, Lucy McDonald, Hannah Miles, Jane Montgomery, Suzy Pelta, Annie Rigg, Angela Romeo, Tristan Stephenson, Milli Taylor, Nicki Trench, Lily Vanilli and Laura Washburn. All other text by Katherine Bebo copyright © Ryland Peters & Small 2019.

Design & commissioned photography copyright © Ryland Peters & Small 2019 (see page 160 for a full list of credits).

ISBN: 978-1-78879-163-2

Printed in China

A CIP record for this book is available from the British Library.

US Library of Congress Cataloging-in-Publication Data has been applied for.

Notes

• Both British (Metric) and American (Imperial plus US cups) measurements are included in these recipes for your convenience; however it is important to work with only one set of measurements and not alternate between the two within a recipe.

• All spoon measurements are level unless otherwise specified.

• Uncooked or partially cooked eggs should not be served to the very old, frail, young children, pregnant women or those with compromised immune systems.

• Ovens should be preheated to the specified temperatures. We recommend using an oven thermometer. If using a fan-assisted oven, adjust temperatures according to the manufacturer's instructions.

• When a recipe calls for the grated zest of citrus fruit, buy unwaxed fruit and wash well before using. If you can only find treated fruit, scrub well in warm soapy water before using.

• Making ice cream at home – there are many good ice cream machines available. Some contain a freezer unit which enables you to churn ice cream almost instantly and others contain a freezer bowl that requires you to freeze if for about 6–8 hours. If you do not have an ice cream machine, you can still make ice cream at home. Simply place your prepared mixture in a lidded freezerproof box and pop it in the freezer. Remove from the freezer every hour or so, transfer to a large bowl and whisk with an electric hand mixer (or whisk by hand) to incorporate air and break up any large ice crystals. This will help give a light and creamy texture. Repeat this process every hour until the ice cream is frozen. Homemade ice cream will keep well in the freezer for about 2 months. While the recipes on pages 21 and 30 in this book include a homemade ice cream, you can successfully substitute good-quality store-bought versions in a similar flavour if you are short of time.

Contents

Hungry for More

GONE ARE THE DAYS WHEN YOU HAVE TO WAIT A WHOLE WEEK TO FIND OUT WHAT HAPPENS TO YOUR FAVOURITE CHARACTERS IN YOUR MUST-WATCH SHOW. NO MORE CLIFFHANGERS, NO MORE WILL THEY/WON'T THEY? HAND-WRINGING AND NO MORE 'ARGH, I MISSED IT – I THOUGHT IT STARTED AT 7 O'CLOCK!' OUTBURSTS. THESE DAYS, WE ARE FIRMLY IN THE BINGE-WATCHING AGE. SO MUCH SO THAT, IN 2015, THE COLLINS ENGLISH DICTIONARY CHOSE 'BINGE-WATCH' AS THE WORD OF THE YEAR. WE ARE NOW ABLE TO INDULGE IN BACK-TO-BACK-TO-BACK (TO-BACK) EPISODES OF PRETTY MUCH WHATEVER TV SHOW WE DESIRE. OUR VIEWING

PLEASURE IS MAGNIFICENTLY ON-DEMAND, SO WE CAN WITNESS OUR BUDDIES ON THE SMALL SCREEN SAVE THE DAY, FALL IN LOVE, SELF-DESTRUCT AND REACH THE TOP ALL IN ONE SITTING IF THE MOOD STRIKES (AND WE CAN STAY AWAKE). WANT TO HEAR TONY SOPRANO'S NEXT THERAPY BREAKTHROUGH? JUST ONE MORE! NEED TO KNOW IF CARRIE KICKS BIG TO THE CURB? KEEP IT RUNNING! CAN'T WAIT TO FIND OUT WHO DON DRAPER SEDUCES NEXT? DON'T YOU DARE PRESS PAUSE!

WHILE YOU'RE GORGING ON *GAME OF THRONES*, DEVOURING *DEXTER* OR SCARFING DOWN *SCRUBS*, WHAT BETTER WAY TO ENHANCE YOUR DAY/EVENING/NIGHT THAN WITH SOME DELICIOUS FOOD AND DRINK TO COMPLEMENT YOUR SHOW OF CHOICE? ENTER *BINGE-WATCHING EATS*. EACH CHAPTER IN THIS BOOK OUTLINES A SPECIFIC GENRE AND RECOMMENDS VARIOUS

DISHES AND TIPPLES THAT WILL BE THE PERFECT ACCOMPANIMENT TO YOUR BINGE-WATCHING SESH. FORGET NETFLIX AND CHILL — WITH THESE DELIGHTFUL RECIPES, IT'S ALL ABOUT NETFLIX AND FILL. WHATEVER EXCITES YOU ENOUGH TO SIT ON YOUR BACKSIDE FOR HOURS ON END — BE IT COMEDY, FANTASY, POLITICS, CRIME, DRAMA, RETRO SHOWS OR MUSICALS — WE'VE GOT YOU COVERED, AND THEN SOME.

ARE YOU FEELING THE LURE OF YOUR SOFA? IS NETFLIX CALLING? IS IT TIME TO GET YOUR DIGITAL STREAMING ON? BEFORE YOU HUNKER DOWN, FLICK THROUGH THIS BOOK AND DECIDE WHAT YOU'RE GOING TO EAT TO KEEP YOUR HUNGER DOWN — YOU DON'T WANT YOUR GROWLING STOMACH TO INTERRUPT YOUR MARATHON-VIEWING. WARNING: AS YOU'RE CONTEMPLATING WHICH RECIPE TO RUSTLE UP AND WHICH TV SHOW TO DIVE IN TO, THERE MAY BE SOME SPOILERS LURKING (#SORRYNOTSORRY). ONCE YOUR FEAST IS PREPARED, GRAB YOUR 'THANKSGIVING PANTS' (À LA JOEY TRIBBIANI), CLOSE THE CURTAINS, CLIMB UNDER YOUR SLANKET AND PREPARE YOURSELF FOR A SESSION OF SERIOUS SATISFACTION.

IN THE WORDS OF JESSE PINKMAN: BINGE THIS, BITCH!

"YOU KNOW, MAYBE IF YOU EAT MORE COMFORT FOOD YOU
WOULDN'T HAVE TO GO AROUND SHOOTING PEOPLE."
– HUGO 'HURLEY' REYES, *LOST*

Chapter 1

FEATURED SHOWS
*Game of Thrones, Outlander, Dirk Gently's Holistic Detective Agency,
Lost, The X-Files, Stranger Things, Doctor Who.*

OTHER SHOWS
*Black Mirror, Supernatural, The Magicians, Eerie Indiana, The Flash,
Arrow, Once Upon a Time, American Gods, Lucifer, The Originals,
Shadowhunters, Supergirl, Smallville, Westworld, Van Helsing,
Penny Dreadful, Heroes, Charmed.*

Is It Just Fantasy?

THE TASTE IS OUT THERE

HOW DID ROBOT DOGS COME TO TAKE OVER THE WORLD? IS THAT
POLAR BEAR CHARGING ABOUT IN PURGATORY? AND JUST WHY DOES
MULDER LOVE SUNFLOWER SEEDS SO MUCH? FANTASY TV CAN THROW
UP SOME REAL HEAD-SCRATCHERS. YOU'LL NEED BRAIN FOOD TO COME
UP WITH A FEW PLAUSIBLE THEORIES. PERHAPS THESE RECIPES WILL INSPIRE
YOU TO ARRIVE AT ANSWERS ABOUT THE SPACE-TIME CONTINUUM. MAYBE
YOU'LL PUT TOGETHER AN ACTION PLAN ON HOW YOU'D DEFEND YOUR
KINGDOM IN WESTEROS. OR YOU COULD REACH A CONCLUSION ABOUT
WHETHER OR NOT WE'RE ALONE IN THE UNIVERSE. BUT THERE'S THE
CHANCE THAT THEY'LL SIMPLY ENCOURAGE YOU TO SIT BACK, EAT, AND
WATCH ALL THE MIND-BENDING CRAZINESS UNFOLD WHILE YOU'RE
PULLED INTO A BLACK HOLE OF DELICIOUSNESS.

Lemon Cake

CHANNEL YOUR INNER SANSA STARK AND SETTLE DOWN FOR AN EVENING OF ZINGY ESCAPISM WITH *GAME OF THRONES*. LEMON CAKES ARE SANSA'S FAVOURITE, AND A PREFERRED TREAT FOR THE NOBLEWOMEN OF THE SEVEN KINGDOMS.

225 g/2 sticks unsalted butter, softened
250 g/1 cup clear honey
100 g/½ cup dark muscovado sugar
250 g/2 cups self-raising/self-rising flour
3 UK large (US extra-large) eggs
50 ml/3½ tablespoons London dry gin

TOPPING
200 g/1⅔ cups icing/confectioners' sugar
grated zest of 1 lemon

a 20-cm/8-inch loose-bottomed cake pan, greased

SERVES 10–12

Preheat the oven to 160°C (325°F) Gas 3.

Put the butter, honey and sugar in a saucepan set over a gentle heat and melt slowly. Bring to the boil for a minute, then remove from the heat and set aside to cool for about 15 minutes.

Sift the flour into a large mixing bowl and beat in the eggs. Add the honey mixture and stir in, then add the gin and keep stirring. Don't worry if it looks a little runny – just so long as it's smooth.

Pour the mixture into the prepared cake pan and bake in the preheated oven for 50–60 minutes. Do the skewer test; if it comes out clean, then you're home dry. If not, give the cake a little more time in the oven, but you may want to lay a sheet of kitchen foil over the top of the cake to stop it from getting too much colour. When cooked through, remove from the oven and turn out onto a wire rack to cool completely.

To make the topping, add a few drops of water to the icing/confectioners' sugar and mix to a spreadable consistency. Spoon the icing over the cake, decorate with a sprinkling of lemon zest and leave to set.

Scottish Oatcakes

TRANSPORT YOURSELF TO THE SCOTTISH HIGHLANDS WITH THESE CRUMBLY OATCAKES, THEN HEAD OVER TO FRANCE (WHERE THE SECOND SEASON OF *OUTLANDER* IS SET) WHEN YOU TOP THEM WITH A WONDERFULLY SMELLY FRENCH CHEESE. A SATISFIED SIGH IS DEFINITELY IN YOUR FUTURE (OR IS IT YOUR PAST?).

200 g/1½ cups rolled/old-fashioned oats
80 g/⅔ cup plain/all-purpose flour, sifted, plus extra for dusting
1 teaspoon bicarbonate of soda/baking soda
1 teaspoon salt
1 teaspoon sugar
80 g/5 tablespoons butter, chilled and cubed
80 ml/⅓ cup warm milk

a 7.5-cm/3-inch round cookie cutter
a baking sheet, greased and lined with non-stick baking paper

MAKES 16

Preheat the oven to 180°C (350°F) Gas 4.

Put the oats, flour, bicarbonate of soda/baking soda, salt and sugar in a large mixing bowl. Rub the butter into the oat mixture using your fingertips. Add the milk and bring the mixture together into a firm dough, adding a little more milk if the mixture is too dry.

On a flour-dusted surface, roll out the dough thinly and stamp out circles using the cookie cutter, re-rolling the trimmings as necessary. (You should re-roll the dough only once as it will become crumbly with the extra flour and difficult to roll.)

Arrange the oatcakes on the prepared baking sheet a small distance apart and bake in the preheated oven for 15 minutes, then turn over and cook for a further 5–10 minutes until crisp and lightly golden brown. Leave to cool on the baking sheet for a few minutes, then transfer to a wire rack to cool completely.

The oatcakes will keep for up to 5 days in an airtight container.

Tawnies

IS IT A TART? IS IT A BROWNIE? WHO KNOWS! WHO CARES! IT'S DELICIOUS, ALL THE SAME. IN THE ZANY WORLD OF *DIRK GENTLY'S HOLISTIC DETECTIVE AGENCY*, WHERE NOTHING IS QUITE WHAT IT SEEMS, NAVIGATE THIS MASH-UP OF TWO SWEET TREATS, JUST AS DIRK NAVIGATES A CONFUDDLING MURDER CASE.

100 g/6½ tablespoons butter
80 g/⅔ cup icing/confectioners' sugar
a small pinch of salt
210 g/1⅔ cups plain/all-purpose flour
1 vanilla pod/bean, split in half lengthwise and seeds scraped out
2 egg yolks
1 tablespoon cold full-fat/whole milk

BROWNIE FILLING
150 g/5 oz. dark/bittersweet chocolate, roughly chopped
75 g/5 tablespoons unsalted butter
150 g/¾ cup light muscovado sugar
2 eggs, beaten
2 balls of Chinese stem ginger, finely chopped
finely grated zest of 1 orange
a pinch of salt
55 g/scant ½ cup rice flour
½ teaspoon baking powder
1 teaspoon ground ginger

8 x 10-cm/4-inch individual tart pans

MAKES 8

Cream together the butter, icing/confectioners' sugar and salt before rubbing in the flour, vanilla seeds and egg yolks – you can do this by hand or in a food processor. When the mixture looks like coarse breadcrumbs, add the milk. Work the mixture gently until you have formed a dough. Wrap the dough in clingfilm/plastic wrap and pop it in the fridge for 1 hour.

Preheat the oven to 180°C (350°F) Gas 4.

Roll the pastry between two sheets of clingfilm/plastic wrap (this will prevent you from needing to use excess flour) to the thickness of 3 mm/⅛ inch and line the tart pans with it. Prick the pastry bases with a fork, and line with baking parchment and baking beans. Bake for 5–10 minutes, making sure the pastry edges don't brown too quickly. Remove the paper and baking beans, and bake for another 5 minutes, or until the base is lightly golden. Leave the tart cases on a wire rack to cool.

To make the brownie filling, place the chocolate and butter in a heatproof bowl suspended over a pan of barely simmering water. Stir every now and then until the chocolate and butter have melted. Stir in the sugar and remove the bowl from the heat. Whisk in the beaten eggs, stem ginger and orange zest, before sifting over the salt, rice flour, baking powder and ground ginger. Fold in until fully combined and divide the mixture between the pastry cases.

Bake for 5 minutes, before turning the oven down to 140°C (275°F) Gas 1 and bake for a further 5–7 minutes. Leave to cool slightly before removing the tawnies from their pans.

Island Poke

FILMED ON A TROPICAL HAWAIIAN ISLAND, *LOST* POSES MORE QUESTIONS THAN IT ANSWERS. TRY NOT TO GET TOO BOGGED DOWN WITH IT ALL – INSTEAD, IMAGINE YOU'RE LOLLING UNDER A PALM TREE, UMBRELLA'D COCKTAIL IN HAND, INDULGING IN THIS TRADITIONAL HAWAIIAN DISH. ALOHA!

600 g/1 lb. 5 oz. fresh or sashimi-grade fish (tuna is classic, but to avoid eating over-fished tuna, you can substitute any other sashimi-grade fish)

½ teaspoon sugar

3 tablespoons soy sauce

1 tablespoon sesame oil

1 tablespoon grated fresh ginger

1 tablespoon finely chopped red chilli/chile

35 g/½ cup (about 5) chopped spring onions/scallions

1 tablespoon black sesame seeds

1 tablespoon white sesame seeds

1 large avocado, diced into 1-cm/½-inch dice

1 head iceberg lettuce or thick cucumber slices, slightly hollowed out, to serve

SERVES 6–8

Trim any sinew or bloodlines off the fish. Cut the flesh into 1-cm/½-inch dice.

Stir the sugar into the soy sauce until it dissolves. Mix with the sesame oil, ginger and chilli/chile. Combine the soy dressing with the fish. Gently fold through the spring onions/scallions, sesame seeds and avocado.

Serve with lettuce leaves to wrap around or pile onto thick slices of cucumber.

To make this dish heartier, serve with warm sticky rice made just before serving.

Sunflower Seed Popcorn

IN-BETWEEN CRACKING CASES OF THE PARANORMAL KIND, SPECIAL AGENT FOX MULDER TAKES GREAT PLEASURE IN CRACKING SUNFLOWER SEEDS WITH HIS TEETH IN *THE X-FILES*. HE CAN'T GET ENOUGH OF THEM – AND YOU WON'T BE ABLE TO GET ENOUGH OF THIS SUPER-SEEDY POPCORN. OR TRY THE SPICY VARIATION INSPIRED BY SCULLY'S RED TRESSES!

3–4 tablespoons pumpkin seed oil, plus extra for drizzling
90 g/⅓ cup popcorn kernels
5 tablespoons toasted sunflower or pumpkin seeds
sea salt and freshly ground black pepper

MAKES I LARGE BOWL

Heat the oil in a large lidded saucepan with a few popcorn kernels in the pan. When you hear the kernels pop, carefully tip in the rest of the kernels. Shake the pan over the heat until the popping stops. Take care when lifting the lid as any unpopped kernels may pop from the heat of the pan. Stir the popcorn well so that it is evenly coated in the oil, drizzling over a little more oil if necessary. Tip the popcorn into a bowl, removing any unpopped kernels as you go.

Sprinkle the toasted seeds over the popcorn, season with a good crunch of salt and pepper (about a teaspoon of each) and stir well. Serve warm or cold.

Variation (see picture on front cover)
Spicy Popcorn – replace the pumpkin seed oil with sunflower oil, follow the method as above but sprinkle with ½ teaspoon salt, ½ teaspoon smoked paprika and ¼ teaspoon cayenne pepper.

Peanut Waffles
with Snickers Ice Cream

ONE BITE OF THIS MOUTH-WATERING WAFFLE TOPPED WITH AN OOZY SNICKERS SAUCE AND THERE'S EVERY CHANCE YOU'LL BECOME AS OBSESSED WITH IT AS ELEVEN IN *STRANGER THINGS* IS WITH EGGO WAFFLES. L'EGGO MY EGGO.

Begin by preparing the sauce. Place the cream, Snickers bars and honey in a saucepan or pot set over a medium heat and simmer until the Snickers bars have melted and the sauce is glossy. Set aside to cool.

For the ice cream, put the double/heavy cream and milk in a saucepan or pot set over a high heat and bring to the boil. In a mixing bowl, whisk together the egg yolks and caster/granulated sugar until very thick and pale yellow in colour. Pour the hot milk over the eggs in a thin stream, whisking all the time. Add the peanut butter and whisk again. Return the mixture to the pan and cook for a few minutes longer, until it begins to thicken. Leave to cool completely.

225 g/1¾ cups self-raising/self-rising flour, sifted
1 teaspoon baking powder
2 tablespoons caster/granulated sugar
pinch of salt
3 eggs, separated
400 ml/1⅔ cups milk
2 tablespoons smooth peanut butter
100 g/7 tablespoons butter, melted

SNICKERS SAUCE
400 ml/1⅔ cups double/heavy cream
6 Snickers bars or other nut, caramel and nougat chocolate bar, chopped
2 teaspoons clear honey

PEANUT BUTTER ICE CREAM
400 ml/1⅔ cups double/heavy cream
200 ml/¾ cup milk
5 egg yolks
100 g/½ cup caster/granulated sugar
2 tablespoons peanut butter (crunchy or smooth)

an electric or stove-top waffle iron
an ice cream machine (optional, see note on page 4)

SERVES 8

Then churn in an ice cream machine following the manufacturer's instructions or if you don't have an ice cream machine, see note on page 4. Once the ice cream is almost frozen, but still soft enough to stir, stir through about one-third of the Snickers sauce so that it is rippled through the ice cream. Transfer to a freezer-proof container and store in the freezer until you are ready to serve.

To make the waffle batter, put the flour, baking powder, caster/granulated sugar, salt, egg yolks, milk, peanut butter and melted butter in a large mixing bowl. Whisk until you have a smooth batter. In a separate mixing bowl, whisk the egg whites to stiff peaks and then gently fold into the batter one-third at a time.

Preheat the waffle iron and grease with a little butter.

Ladle a small amount of the batter into the preheated waffle iron and cook the waffles for 2–3 minutes until golden brown. Keep the waffles warm while you cook the remaining batter in the same way.

Serve the waffles immediately with the ice cream and remaining Snickers sauce.

Fish Finger Sandwich
with Tartare Sauce

REJOICE WITH THE DOCTOR WHEN HE DISCOVERS HIS LOVE OF FISH FINGERS DIPPED IN CUSTARD. THIS *DOCTOR WHO*-INSPIRED SANDWICH IS SOMEWHAT MORE CONVENTIONAL, BUT NO LESS GRATIFYING. A SIDE OF CUSTARD OPTIONAL, BUT NOT RECOMMENDED (UNLESS YOU'RE AN EXTRATERRESTRIAL TIME LORD).

2 skinned and boned fillets of
   cod or haddock
sunflower or vegetable oil,
   for frying

BEER BATTER
200 g/1½ cups plain/all-purpose
   flour
2 teaspoons sea salt
2 x 330-ml/11-fl. oz. bottles
   of lager

TARTARE SAUCE
225 g/1 cup mayonnaise
80 g/½ cup pickles/gherkins
1 teaspoon capers, chopped
2 teaspoons Dijon mustard
2 teaspoons chopped shallots
2 tablespoons chopped spring
   onions/scallions
2 teaspoons lemon juice
Tabasco sauce, to taste
sea salt and freshly ground
   black pepper

TO SERVE
French country bread
butter, for spreading
handful of cos/romaine lettuce
   leaves, cut into strips
fries

MAKES 2

Prepare your fish for battering. If the fish isn't already skinned and boned, do so. Slice the fish into 6 finger-size strips.

For the batter, whisk together the flour, salt and lager in a bowl until combined.

Fill a large frying pan/skillet with about 2.5 cm/1 inch oil over a high heat, but don't leave this unattended. When the oil is bubbling steadily, it's ready to go. Dip the fish fingers in the batter, remove any excess and then lower carefully into the oil using tongs, if necessary. Fry for about 4 minutes on each side over a moderate heat until golden and crispy.

Remove the fish fingers carefully from the oil and drain well on paper towels. Season with sea salt.

Mix all the ingredients for the tartare sauce together in a mixing bowl.

Cut the French country bread into thick slices. Lay one down and butter it before spreading a couple of tablespoons of tartare sauce on top. Place 3 fish fingers on top, then a few strips of lettuce, before placing a second slice of bread on top.

Serve with fries.

"PLAY WITH YOUR FOOD, MASON, AND GIVE IT
THE OPPORTUNITY TO BITE BACK."
— ALANA BLOOM, *HANNIBAL*

Chapter 2

FEATURED SHOWS
*Hannibal, Bates Motel, Killing Eve, Dexter,
The Walking Dead, True Blood.*

OTHER SHOWS
*Scream, Buffy the Vampire Slayer, The Sinner, Evil Genius,
The Vampire Diaries, iZombie, Santa Clarita Diet, Slasher,
The Returned, Grimm, The Strain, Fringe, American Horror
Story, The Terror, The ABC Murders, Evil Lives Here.*

Murder & Mayhem

KILLED IT!

ARE YOU HUNGRY FOR HORROR? FAMISHED FOR FEAR? STARVING FOR SHOCK? COULD YOU MURDER A STEAK/PECAN PIE/BLOODY MARY? THEN LOOK NO FURTHER THAN THIS FRIGHTFULLY FLAVOURFUL CHAPTER, WHICH DELVES INTO THE MURKY MINDS — AND EATING HABITS — OF SERIAL KILLERS, OBSESSIVE ODDBALLS AND PSYCHOTIC ASSASSINS. OH, WITH A FEW VAMPIRES AND ZOMBIES THROWN INTO THE MIX. DURING FRIGHT NIGHT, THERE'S BLOOD, THERE'S GORE, THERE'S AN UNSUSPECTING MOTHER... AND, MOST IMPORTANTLY, THERE'S A BLOODY ENTICING ARRAY OF APPETIZING BITES. IF ALL THAT FEAR ISN'T ENOUGH TO PUT YOU OFF YOUR FOOD, GET YOUR FANGS INTO THESE DISHES AND ENJOY YOURSELF A KILLER SPREAD.

Fillet Steak on Toasted Ciabatta

NOTHING SETS OFF AN EVENING OF WATCHING A CANNIBALISTIC SERIAL KILLER BETTER THAN A PLATE OF RARE FLESH. WASHED DOWN WITH A GLUG OR TWO OF CHIANTI, EAT YOUR HEART OUT, HANNIBAL LECTER (WHICH, GIVEN HALF THE CHANCE, HE ACTUALLY WOULD).

1 ciabatta loaf
2 tablespoons wholegrain mustard
2 tablespoons homemade mayonnaise or good-quality prepared mayonnaise
400 g/14 oz. beef fillet
1 tablespoon olive oil
50 g/2 oz. rocket/arugula
sea salt and freshly ground black pepper

a griddle/grill pan

MAKES ABOUT 20

Preheat the oven to 200°C (400°F) Gas 6.

Cut the ciabatta loaf in half lengthways and toast in the oven for about 10 minutes. Mix the mustard and mayonnaise together and spread evenly onto the cut sides of the toasted ciabatta.

Brush the beef with the olive oil and heat a griddle/grill pan. Sear the beef in the hot pan without disturbing, for about 2 minutes, and repeat on the other side. Transfer the beef to a chopping board and let it rest for 15 minutes.

Using a sharp knife, slice the beef into enough thin slices to cover the ciabatta. Press the beef gently onto the ciabatta, to encourage it to stick to the mustard mixture. Scatter the rocket/arugula over the beef and carefully cut into fingers. Serve with little dishes of sea salt and cracked black pepper on the side.

Meringue Bones with Cherry Sauce

NORMAN BATES IS ONE SINISTER DUDE. LET THESE MORBID MERINGUE BONES MELT IN YOUR MOUTH AS YOU WITNESS HIM BECOMING MORE AND MORE OBSESSED WITH HIS MOTHER IN *BATES MOTEL*, WHILE PONDERING, 'DOES SHE HAVE ANY IDEA WHAT GRISLY FATE AWAITS HER?'

3 UK large/US extra-large egg
   whites, at room temperature
½ teaspoon lemon juice
a pinch of salt
140/⅔ cup caster/superfine
   sugar

CHERRY SAUCE
125 g/1 cup canned black
   cherries, juice reserved
50 g/¼ cup caster/superfine
   sugar
120 ml/½ cup juice from the
   canned cherries
½ teaspoon lemon juice
1 tablespoon cornflour/
   cornstarch

*3–4 baking sheets, lined with
   baking parchment*

MAKES ABOUT 18

Preheat the oven to 100°C (212°F) Gas 1.

In a medium bowl and using an electric mixer, beat the egg whites, lemon juice and salt until fluffy, starting on a low speed and gradually increasing until soft peaks form. Gradually beat in the sugar, 2 tablespoons at a time, and continue beating on a high speed until stiff peaks form. Spoon the mixture into a piping/pastry bag fitted with a number 10 nozzle/tip.

Pipe 15-cm/6-inch bone shapes onto the prepared baking sheets, starting at the round edge of the bone and working your way down to make the length, and finishing on the round of the opposite side. Repeat in reverse to make a crisscross, ensuring there are no weak spots where the meringue is too thin.

Bake in the preheated oven for 1 hour or until set. Turn off the oven and leave inside the cooling oven to dry for 1 hour. Store in airtight containers if making in advance.

To make the sauce, blend the cherries in a food processor, transfer to a saucepan and add all the other ingredients. Bring to the boil, stirring constantly then reduce the heat and simmer until the mixture has thickened to the desired consistency. Allow to cool. Trickle over the bones or serve alongside as a dip.

Strawberry Shortcake Sundae

ONLY A TRUE PSYCHOPATH WOULD WANT TO WASTE ICE CREAM. WATCH IN HORROR AS *KILLING EVE'S* ENTRANCING PROTAGONIST MALICIOUSLY KNOCKS AN ICE CREAM SUNDAE INTO A LITTLE GIRL'S LAP. THEN CONSOLE YOURSELF WITH THIS ONE AS YOU FOLLOW THIS ASSASSIN'S MURDEROUS MOVES.

400 g/14 oz. fresh strawberries, hulled and sliced
250 ml/1 cup double/heavy cream, whipped
4 shortcake fan cookies, to serve

STRAWBERRY & CLOTTED CREAM ICE CREAM
160 g/generous ¾ cup caster/ superfine sugar
2 UK large/US extra-large eggs
225 g/8 oz. clotted cream
250 ml/1 cup double/heavy cream
250 ml/1 cup full-fat/whole milk
400 g/14 oz. fresh strawberries, hulled and chopped

SUMMER BERRY SAUCE
1 vanilla pod/bean or 1 teaspoon pure vanilla extract
250 g/9 oz. fresh strawberries
150 g/5 oz. fresh raspberries
100 g/½ cup caster/superfine sugar

an ice cream machine (optional, see note on page 4)

SERVES 4

To make the Strawberry & Clotted Cream Ice Cream, put the sugar, eggs, clotted cream, double/heavy cream, milk and strawberries in a blender. Blitz for a few minutes until you have a smooth mixture. Churn in an ice cream machine according to the manufacturer's instructions, or freeze using the by-hand method given on page 4. Freeze until needed.

To make the Summer Berry Sauce, cut the vanilla pod/bean in half lengthways using a sharp knife. Place all the ingredients in a saucepan with 200 ml/¾ cup water and simmer for 8–10 minutes until the strawberries are very soft and the sugar has dissolved. Strain the sauce through a fine mesh sieve/strainer, pressing the fruit down to release all the juices. Discard the fruit and leave the sauce to cool before using.

To assemble the sundaes, put a generous layer of sliced strawberries and Summer Berry Sauce in each sundae dish. Add a scoop of Strawberry & Clotted Cream Ice Cream, follow with a large dollop of whipped cream and finish with another scoop of the ice cream. Drizzle with the remaining sauce, decorate with a shortcake fan cookie and serve immediately.

Bloody Mary Granitas

IN THE WORDS OF THE SERIAL-KILLING, BLOOD-SPATTER ANALYST *DEXTER*, "BLOOD NEVER LIES". THESE BLOOD-RED, CHILLING TREATS WOULD CERTAINLY APPEAL TO HIS DARK PASSENGER, AS WELL AS HIS NEMESIS THE ICE TRUCK KILLER, WHO DISCOVERS THAT BLOOD ISN'T ALWAYS THICKER THAN WATER. NO LIE.

7–8 tomatoes, skinned and roughly chopped
450 ml/scant 2 cups tomato juice
100 ml/⅓ cup vodka
1 tablespoon Worcestershire sauce
freshly squeezed juice of 1 lime
1 teaspoon celery salt
1 teaspoon finely grated onion
hot pepper sauce, such as Tabasco, to taste
sea salt and freshly ground black pepper
celery stick/stalk or fronds, to garnish

MAKES 4–6

Put the tomatoes in a food processor and whizz until smooth. Add the tomato juice and vodka and whizz again. Next, add the Worcestershire sauce, lime juice, celery salt and onion, whizz, then check the seasoning, adding salt, pepper and hot pepper sauce to taste.

Pour into a shallow plastic box and freeze for about 1½ hours. Rough up the surface with a fork and freeze for another 45 minutes. Fork through again and freeze for another 45 minutes if serving straight away or freeze until hard if making ahead, in which case mellow in the fridge for 30 minutes before serving.

Spoon into glasses and garnish with a celery stick or a few fronds, as preferred. Serve with small spoons.

Zombie Hands Cupcakes

AS YOU SIT, TRANSFIXED BY THE NAIL-BITING HORROR SERIES *THE WALKING DEAD*, IT COULD BE A CASE OF DEATH BY CHOCOLATE WITH THESE POST-APOCALYPTIC ZOMBIE CAKES. THEY REALLY ARE FINGER-LICKING GOOD AND TOTALLY NAIL FRIGHTFUL FLAVOUR.

60 g/¼ cup butter, softened
140 g/⅔ cup caster/granulated sugar
1 egg
½ teaspoon pure vanilla extract
115 g/¾ cup plain/all-purpose flour
80 g/¾ cup unsweetened cocoa powder
¼ teaspoon bicarbonate of soda/ baking soda
80 ml/⅓ cup sour cream
4 tablespoons espresso, cooled
1 quantity Chocolate Fudge Frosting, omit the chilli/chile syrup (see page 89)
150 g/5½ oz. marzipan
2 teaspoons icing/confectioners' sugar
flaked/sliced almonds, to decorate

MAKES 6 OR 12, AS PREFERRED

Preheat the oven to 180°C (350°F) Gas 4. Line a 12-hole (or 6-hole) muffin pan with paper cases, as preferred.

Using an electric mixer, cream the butter and sugar together until very light and fluffy (about 5 minutes). Add the egg and vanilla extract and beat until thoroughly incorporated.

Sift the flour, 30 g/¼ cup of the cocoa and the baking soda into a mixing bowl. Add these dry ingredients to the butter and sugar mixture in three parts, alternating with the sour cream, then slowly add the cooled coffee. Use an ice cream scoop to spoon the batter into the prepared muffin pan.

Bake in the preheated oven for about 15 minutes, until a toothpick inserted into the centre comes out clean. Cool in the pan for a few minutes, then transfer to a wire rack to cool completely.

To decorate, spread the top of the cupcakes with Chocolate Fudge Frosting, then dust with a thick layer of the remaining cocoa powder. Roll out the marzipan to the size and shape of your fingers. Insert a toothpick into each finger as far as you need to in order to make it stand upright and hold the shape you want. Mix the sugar with a few drops of water and use to stick an almond flake to the end of each finger. Secure the fingers into the top of the cake.

Pecan Pie

SOB ALONG WITH SOOKIE IN *TRUE BLOOD* AS SHE SITS AND EATS A PECAN PIE — THE LAST THING HER GRAN COOKED BEFORE SHE DIED. IT'S HEARTBREAKING, NUTTY STUFF. THEN CHEER YOURSELF UP BY FAST-FORWARDING TO A SCENE WHERE JASON HAS HIS SHIRT OFF.

500-g/1-lb. 2 oz. block of shortcrust pastry, chilled
75 g/5 tablespoons unsalted butter
225 g/1 cup plus 2 tablespoons light muscovado sugar
325 g/1⅓ cups maple syrup
½ teaspoon salt
225 g/1½ cups pecans
2 tablespoons bourbon
2 teaspoons pure vanilla extract
3 eggs, lightly beaten

a 23-cm/9-in. loose-bottomed tart pan

SERVES 8–10

Preheat the oven to 180°C (350°F) Gas 4.

Roll the pastry between two sheets of clingfilm/plastic wrap until it is about 1 cm/½ inch thick. Take off the top layer of clingfilm/plastic wrap and upturn the pastry into the tart pan. Gently press the pastry into the edges of the pan, slicing the overhanging edges off with your thumb. Remove the top layer of clingfilm/plastic wrap and prick the base with a fork. Put the tart case in the freezer for 15 minutes to chill.

Line the pastry case with baking parchment and fill with baking beans. Bake in the oven for 15 minutes. Remove the baking beans and baking parchment and return to the oven for 5 minutes more.

While the pastry case is baking, make the filling. Put the butter, sugar, maple syrup and salt in a saucepan and stir over a medium heat until the butter has melted and the sugar has dissolved. Turn the heat up and bring the mixture to the boil. Take the pan off the heat and mix in the pecans, bourbon and vanilla, and leave to cool for a few minutes. Whisk the eggs into the slightly cooled mixture until completely combined and pour the filling into the tart case. Bake for 40–45 minutes.

Leave the pie to cool in its pan on a wire rack before unmoulding. Serve warm or at room temperature.

"HAVE A DRINK. IT'LL MAKE ME LOOK YOUNGER."
— ROGER STERLING, *MAD MEN*

Chapter 3

FEATURED SHOWS
*Peaky Blinders, Boardwalk Empire, Happy Days,
Mad Men, That 70s Show, The Americans.*

OTHER SHOWS
*Dynasty, Dallas, I Love Lucy, Bewitched, The Brady Bunch,
The Wonder Years, Leave it to Beaver, Lassie, That Girl, Route 66,
The Little Rascals, Chips, I Dream of Jeannie, Saved by the Bell,
Wonder Woman, The A-Team, Mork & Mindy.*

Go Retro

BYGONE BITES

FLASHBACK ALERT! THIS CHAPTER STARTS IN 1919 WITH THOSE HARD-AS-NAILS *Peaky Blinders*, THEN TAKES YOU FOR A MOUTH-WATERING STROLL ALONG *Boardwalk Empire* IN THE 1930S, BEFORE POPPING INTO AL'S DINER FROM *Happy Days* IN THE ROCKIN' 'N' ROLLIN' 1950S. THEN IT'S OFF TO THE ULTRA-COOL ADVERTISING WORLD OF 1960S NEW YORK WITH THOSE COCKTAIL-SWILLING *Mad Men*, BEFORE HANGING OUT IN THE 1970S AMONGST ALL THE GLITTER BALLS, FLARES AND, ER, PRAWN/SHRIMP COCKTAILS IN *That '70s Show*. OUR FINAL RETRO STOP IS THE 1980S WITH *The Americans*, WHO ARE JUST TRYING TO BLEND IN (WHILE KICKING SOME SERIOUS BUTT). WHEN IT COMES TO A CULINARY TRIP DOWN MEMORY LANE, ONE THING'S FOR SURE — GOOD FOOD AND DRINK NEVER GO OUT OF STYLE.

Blood & Sand

THIS GANGSTER-APPROVED COCKTAIL IS THE PERFECT TIPPLE TO STEADY YOUR NERVES AS YOU WATCH ALFIE IN *PEAKY BLINDERS* GET SHOT BY TOMMY ON THE BEACH. THERE'S BLOOD, THERE'S SAND AND, AFTER TOMMY LEAVES THE SCENE OF THE CRIME, CHANCES ARE HE'LL KNOCK BACK A WHISKEY OR TWO.

35 ml/1¼ fl. oz. Dewar's White Label
35 ml/1¼ fl. oz. Cherry Heering Liqueur
35 ml/1¼ fl. oz. Martini Rosso Vermouth
35 ml/1¼ fl. oz. fresh orange juice
ice cubes

MAKES 1

Put a martini glass in the freezer to chill while you make the drink.

Fill a cocktail shaker with ice cubes. Add all of the ingredients and shake for a few seconds until the shaker is frosted. Strain into the chilled martini glass and serve immediately.

The Bee's Knees & Gin Rickey

TURN YOUR LIVING ROOM INTO A SPEAKEASY BY MIXING YOURSELF UP THESE GIN-BASED COCKTAILS AND TUNING INTO *BOARDWALK EMPIRE*, SET DURING THE TIME OF PROHIBITION. SIP AWAY AS YOU WATCH THE DRAMA UNFOLD AROUND NUCKY, THE BOARDWALK AND A WHOLE LOTTA BOOTLEG LIQUOR.

THE BEE'S KNEES
4 tablespoons clear honey
4 tablespoons hot water
90 ml/3 fl. oz. gin
1 tablespoon freshly squeezed
 lemon juice
1 tablespoon freshly squeezed
 orange juice
ice cubes
lemon twists, to serve

SERVES 4

GIN RICKEY
60 ml/2 fl. oz. freshly squeezed
 lime juice
235 ml/8 fl. oz. London dry gin
2 limes, halved
club soda/soda water
ice cubes

SERVES 4

The Bee's Knees
Mix the honey and hot water together to make a syrup. Combine all the ingredients and shake well with ice. Strain into a martini or rocks glass and serve with a twist.

Gin Rickey
Fill four highball glasses full of ice. Pour equal amounts of lime juice into each glass. Add the gin to each glass, throw in a lime half, and top up with bubbly water of choice.

Blue Moon Milkshake

PICTURE THIS: IT'S 1955, YOU'RE SITTING IN AL'S DINER DISCUSSING THE SOCK HOP YOU JITTERBUGGED AT LAST NIGHT WHEN A DUDE IN A LEATHER JACKET COMES IN AND THUMPS THE JUKEBOX. *BLUE MOON* STARTS PLAYING AND THE FONZ HIMSELF BRINGS OVER ONE OF THESE SUPER-COOL MILKSHAKES. *HAPPY DAYS!*

2 tablespoons blueberry syrup
200 ml/¾ cup blue Curaçao
100 ml/⅓ cup full-fat/whole milk
2 scoops Blueberry Ice Cream
  (see below and note on
  page 4)
canned whipped cream
a handful of fresh blueberries,
  to decorate

BLUEBERRY ICE CREAM
1 quantity basic ice cream base
  made without the peanut
  butter (see page 21) or use
  store-bought vanilla ice cream
200 g/1½ cups fresh or frozen
  blueberries
2 tablespoons caster/granulated
  sugar

SERVES 2

Begin by making the Blueberry Ice Cream. Prepare the ice cream base following the recipe for Peanut Butter Ice Cream on page 21, but omit the peanut butter. Put the blueberries, sugar and 2 tablespoons water in a saucepan over a gentle heat. Stir until the sugar has dissolved, then increase the heat until the blueberries have completely broken down. Pass the blueberries through a fine sieve/strainer and discard the seeds and skins, reserving the juice. Stir this juice into the prepared ice cream base and finish following the instructions on page 21.

Place two glasses in the freezer to chill for a few minutes.

Spoon 1 tablespoon of blueberry syrup in the base of each glass. Blend the blue curaçao, milk and Blueberry Ice Cream together until smooth and thick. Divide the milkshake between the glasses. Top with a squirt of cream and add a few fresh blueberries to decorate.

Ranch Dip with Sweet Potato Chips

IF YOU RECEIVED A CHIP 'N' DIP DISH AS A WEDDING GIFT, WHAT WOULD YOU DO? IF YOU WERE PETE CAMPBELL IN *MAD MEN*, YOU'D EXCHANGE IT FOR A GUN AFTER ENDURING MUCH TEASING FROM YOUR COLLEAGUES. THIS CREAMY DIP WILL CERTAINLY GIVE YOU MORE BANG FOR YOUR BUCK.

60 ml/¼ cup buttermilk
150 g/5½ oz. cream cheese
40 ml/2½ tablespoons mayonnaise
1 garlic clove, peeled and chopped
1 tablespoon olive oil
freshly squeezed juice of ½ lemon
1 tablespoon freshly snipped chives
1 tablespoon freshly chopped parsley
1 tablespoon freshly chopped dill
½ teaspoon paprika
1 teaspoon Dijon mustard
sea salt and freshly ground black pepper

SWEET POTATO CHIPS
2 sweet potatoes
2 tablespoons sunflower oil

a baking sheet, lightly greased

SERVES 6–8

In a bowl, whisk together the buttermilk, cream cheese and mayonnaise until smooth.

Put the garlic, olive oil, lemon juice, chives, parsley and dill in a food processor and blitz until very finely chopped and the oil has emulsified. Make sure that there are no large pieces of garlic.

Fold the herb oil into the cream cheese mixture with the paprika and mustard, mixing well so that it is all combined. Season with sea salt and black pepper. Spoon into a serving bowl.

For the chips, preheat the oven to 180°C (350°F) Gas 4. Using a mandoline or sharp knife, finely slice the sweet potato and pat dry. Toss the slices in sunflower oil and season with salt and pepper. Spread the veg on a lightly oiled baking sheet and bake for 10–15 minutes, then turn and bake for 5 minutes more, or until crisp. Transfer to a wire rack to cool. Serve with an extra sprinkling of sea salt.

Variation
Cheddar, bacon and onion ranch dip: Fry 4 rashers/slices of lean bacon until crisp, then chop into small pieces. Allow to cool and stir into the dip (omitting the dill from the original recipe), along with 4 tablespoons grated/shredded cheddar cheese. Garnish with a handful of chopped spring onions/scallions and serve with giant pretzels for dipping.

Prawn & Avocado Cocktail

WE HAVE THE 1970S TO THANK FOR MANY A CULINARY TREND: QUICHES, DEVILLED EGGS, BLACK FOREST GATEAU AND, INDEED, THE TANGY PRAWN/SHRIMP COCKTAIL. GO TO TOWN ON THIS SHELLFISH APPETIZER AS YOU WATCH THE ANTICS OF POLYESTER-CLAD JACKIE, KELSO ET AL IN *THAT '70S SHOW*.

180 g/6 oz. raw, peeled prawns/
   shrimp
100 g/3½ oz. peeled cucumber
1 small wedge of onion
1 small tomato
1 heaped tablespoon freshly
   chopped coriander/cilantro,
   plus extra to garnish
125 ml/½ cup tomato ketchup
75 ml/⅓ cup freshly squeezed
   lime juice
125 ml/½ cup freshly squeezed
   orange juice
5 drops Worcestershire sauce
5 drops Tabasco sauce
a pinch of sea salt
a pinch of white pepper

TO SERVE
50 g/2 oz. avocado flesh, finely
   chopped
saltine crackers or tortilla chips

SERVES 4

Bring 250 ml/1 cup water to the boil in a saucepan and add the prawns/shrimp. Cook for 2 minutes or until opaque and cooked through. Remove from the water with a slotted spoon and reserve the cooking water for later. Set both aside to cool.

Meanwhile, finely chop the cucumber, onion and tomato.

In a bowl, mix the prawns/shrimp, 125 ml/½ cup of the reserved cooking water, the cucumber, onion, tomato, coriander/cilantro, tomato ketchup, lime and orange juice, Worcestershire sauce, Tabasco sauce, salt and pepper. Mix well.

To serve, divide the mixture between 4 cocktail glasses or small bowls and top with the avocado. Garnish with a little extra coriander/cilantro and serve with saltine crackers or tortilla chips.

Mama's Meatloaf

WHEN ELIZABETH AND PHILIP SERVE THE QUINTESSENTIAL AMERICAN FAMILY DINNER OF THE '80S – MEATLOAF – TO THEIR FBI NEIGHBOUR IN *THE AMERICANS*, THERE'S NO WAY HE CAN GUESS THEY'RE NOT ALL THEY SEEM. OR IS THERE? THEIR SECRET INGREDIENT – HORSERADISH – COULD JUST GIVE THE GAME AWAY.

4 tablespoons olive oil
2 onions, finely chopped
1 carrot, finely chopped
1 celery stick, finely chopped
125 ml/½ cup milk
100 g/2 cups fresh breadcrumbs
75 ml/5 tablespoons ketchup
2 teaspoons Worcestershire
   sauce
1 egg, beaten
30 g/1 cup freshly chopped
   flat leaf parsley
400 g/14 oz. coarsely ground
   beef mince/ground beef
400 g/14 oz. coarsely ground
   pork mince/ground pork
400-g/14-oz. can chopped
   tomatoes
2 teaspoons freshly chopped
   thyme
sea salt and freshly ground
   black pepper

a 25 x 12-cm/10 x 5-inch loaf
   pan, lined with non-stick
   baking paper

SERVES 4

Preheat the oven to 200°C (400°F) Gas 6.

Heat the olive oil in a large sauté pan. Add the onions, carrot and celery, and season. Sauté for 5 minutes then transfer into a large mixing bowl.

In a separate bowl, pour the milk over the breadcrumbs and mix together. Add half the ketchup, the Worcestershire sauce, egg, parsley, breadcrumb mixture and the meats to the large mixing bowl. Gently combine everything with your hands.

Pack the mixture into the lined loaf pan. Mix the tomatoes with the remaining ketchup and pour over the meatloaf. Sprinkle with salt and pepper and the thyme. Bake for 1 hour, remove from the oven and let stand for 10 minutes. Serve the meatloaf in thick slices with mashed potatoes.

"YOU, UH... GONNA EAT THAT?"
– CHRISTOPHER MOLTISANTI, *THE SOPRANOS*

Chapter 4

FEATURED SHOWS
*Breaking Bad, Narcos, The Wire, The Bridge,
The Sopranos, Orange is the New Black.*

OTHER SHOWS
*Luther, Making a Murderer, True Detective, The Killing, Sherlock,
Criminal Minds, NCIS, Hawaii Five-O, Line of Duty, Broadchurch,
Happy Valley, The Fall, CSI, Prime Suspect, White Collar, Unforgotten,
Marcella, How to Get Away with Murder, Bloodline.*

Crime & Punishment

ARRESTINGLY APPETIZING

KEEPING YOUR HEAD ON THE MEAN STREETS OF BALTIMORE,
CONCOCTING A BATCH OF CRYSTAL METH OR BEING A COLUMBIAN
DRUG LORD IS ENOUGH TO MAKE ANYONE HUNGRY. AND WATCHING
SUCH SHENANIGANS ON THE SMALL SCREEN IS HUNGRY WORK, TOO.
WHICH IS WHY THIS CHAPTER IS CHOCK-FULL OF RECIPES THAT ARE
CRIMINALLY DELECTABLE TO ACCOMPANY YOUR RESOLUTE VIEWING
OF ORGANISED CRIME, DISORGANISED COPS AND A WHOLE LOTTA
DRUGS, GUNS, MURDER AND FRIED CHICKEN. WHETHER, FOR YOUR
VIEWING PLEASURE, YOU CHOOSE TO WATCH SOMEONE GET
WHACKED OUT ON NARCOTICS, WHACKED OVER THE HEAD WITH
A BLUNT INSTRUMENT, OR WHACKED BY THE MERCILESS MOB, YOU
HAVE THE RIGHT TO REMAIN SILENT (WHILE STUFFING YOUR FACE).

Double-Baked Chicken Wings

FRIED CHICKEN BECAME AN INTEGRAL PART OF WALTER WHITE'S CRYSTAL METH EMPIRE IN *BREAKING BAD*. RECREATE YOUR VERY OWN LOS POLLOS HERMANOS JOINT AND SERVE THIS CRISPY CHICKEN THAT EVEN KINGPIN GUS FRING WOULD BE PROUD OF. WOULD YOU LIKE 'HIGHS' WITH THAT?

1.8 kg/4 lbs. chicken wings, halved at the joints, tips removed
1 tablespoon garlic powder
1 tablespoon onion powder
1 teaspoon freshly ground black pepper
1½ teaspoons paprika
¼ teaspoon cayenne pepper
40 g/3 tablespoons butter
350 ml/1½ cups hot sauce or Tabasco sauce
250 g/1 cup tomato ketchup
120 ml/½ cup ranch seasoning
120 ml/½ cup soy sauce

2 baking sheets, lined with foil and lightly greased

SERVES 4–6

Preheat the oven to 200°C (400°F) Gas 6.

In a large bowl, combine the garlic, onion powder, pepper, paprika and cayenne pepper. Add the wings and toss in the spice mixture.

Arrange the wings in a single layer on the lined baking sheets. Bake the chicken wings in the preheated oven for about 30 minutes. The skin will begin to turn brown and the meat will begin to loosen from the bone.

While the wings are baking, melt the butter in a medium saucepan over a low heat. Stir in the hot sauce (or Tabasco), ketchup, ranch seasoning and soy sauce. When the wings are done, place them in a large bowl and pour three-quarters of the sauce over them. Toss until covered.

Replace the foil on the baking sheets and rearrange the coated wings back on the sheets.

Bake the wings for a further 5–10 minutes, until the juices run clear when the thickest part is pierced to the bone. You'll have to keep an eye on them now because you will not want to overcook them. Serve with the remaining sauce drizzled over the top.

Empanadillas

NARCOS FOLLOWS THE INCREDIBLE RISE AND FALL OF COLOMBIAN DRUG LORD PABLO ESCOBAR. IT'S HIGHLY ADDICTIVE, AS ARE THESE TASTY PASTRY TURNOVERS POPULAR THROUGHOUT LATIN AMERICA. DEVOUR THEM AS YOU GAPE AT THE UNBELIEVABLE GREED, POWER AND INFLUENCE OF ONE MAN.

125 g/1 stick plus 1 tablespoon
   unsalted butter, chilled
225 g/1¾ cups cups plain/
   all-purpose flour
1 egg, beaten
30 ml/2 tablespoons cold water,
   if needed
¼ teaspoon salt

SPINACH & RICOTTA FILLING
20 g/1 generous tablespoon
   unsalted butter
150 g/5 oz. fresh spinach
1 tablespoon olive oil
½ onion, finely chopped
1 garlic clove, crushed
20 g/1 oz. freshly grated
   Parmesan
½ beaten egg
160 g/5½ oz. ricotta (drained)
a pinch of salt
½ teaspoon freshly grated
   nutmeg

*a 7.5-cm/3-inch round cookie
   cutter*

MAKES 30

Cut the butter into small cubes. Place the butter, flour and half the beaten egg into the food processor and blitz until a dough forms. Add the water if the dough doesn't come together. Wrap the dough in clingfilm/plastic wrap and refrigerate for 30 minutes. Reserve the remaining egg for brushing.

Preheat the oven to 200°C (400°F) Gas 6.

Meanwhile, make the filling. Add the butter to a small saucepan, along with the spinach and a splash of water. Cover and leave to steam for a few minutes. When wilted, drain in a sieve/strainer and chop finely. Place in a large bowl. In the same pan, add the olive oil and sauté the onion and garlic. Add the onion and garlic to the spinach. When cool, add the cheeses and egg. Season with salt and nutmeg.

Roll out the dough to 3 mm/⅛ inch thick. Use the cutter to stamp out disks. Lay the disks out on a lightly floured surface and put a heaped teaspoon of filling in the middle.

Moisten the top half of the dough with a little water. Pull over the other half of dough, taking care to squeeze out any air. You can do this by pressing down on the edge of the dough with the tines of a fork or by folding and pinching the edges over. Place on a baking sheet, brush with a little of the remaining beaten egg and bake in the preheated oven for 15–20 minutes, or until golden.

Mini Crab Cakes
with Chilli Lime Mayo

BALTIMORE'S FAIDLEY SEAFOOD CRAB CAKES ARE SO FAMOUS THEY EVEN MADE IT INTO THE GRITTY CRIME DRAMA *THE WIRE*. MAKE LIKE MCNULTY AND GET PEOPLE TO DO THINGS FOR YOU BY FEEDING THEM THESE CRAB CAKES AND BEER.

500 g/1 lb. 2 oz. cooked/lump white crabmeat
4 spring onions/scallions, finely chopped
1 garlic clove, crushed
1 hot red or green chilli/chile, deseeded and very finely chopped
1 tablespoon freshly chopped flat leaf parsley or coriander/cilantro
1 tablespoon nam pla (or other) fish sauce
1 teaspoon muscovado or light brown sugar
1 egg, beaten
1 teaspoon white wine vinegar
a good pinch of sea salt
plain/all-purpose flour, to dust
125 ml/½ cup sunflower or groundnut/peanut oil, for frying

CHILLI LIME MAYO
4 tablespoons mayonnaise
grated zest and freshly squeezed juice of 1 small lime
1 Scotch Bonnet chilli/chile, very finely chopped

MAKES 16

Mix together the crabmeat, spring onions/scallions, garlic, chilli, fresh herbs, fish sauce, sugar, egg, vinegar and salt. This can most easily be done in a food processor; however mixing by hand in a bowl will give more texture to the final crab cakes. Divide into 16 pieces and shape into balls, then flatten to discs. Dust each crab cake lightly with flour and refrigerate for 30 minutes before cooking. (This makes them easier to handle and less likely to fall apart during cooking.)

Heat the oil in a large frying pan/skillet set over a medium heat and fry the crab cakes in small batches for about 2 minutes each side, until golden.

To make the Chilli Lime Mayo, mix the mayonnaise and lime juice in a small bowl. Add the Scotch Bonnet, little by little, until the desired hotness is achieved. Garnish with grated lime zest. Serve on the side for dipping.

Gravadlax with Pickles on Rye Bread

THE BRIDGE – SET BETWEEN SWEDEN AND DENMARK – IS A TALE OF TWO HALVES. INDULGE IN THIS SCANDINAVIAN DISH OF THREE PARTS AS YOU WATCH THE DETECTIVES TRY TO DISCOVER THE SINISTER TRUTH. ONE THING'S FOR SURE: SOMETHING FISHY IS GOING ON.

buttered dark rye bread, to serve

GRAVADLAX
1 tablespoon juniper berries
1 tablespoon fennel seeds
1 tablespoon black peppercorns
50 g/2 oz. coarse sea salt
4 tablespoons demerara sugar
750 g/1 lb. 10 oz. salmon fillet, 2.5 cm/1 inch thick, pin-boned and scaled

PICKLES
2 cucumbers, sliced 5 mm/¼ inch thick
1 small onion, thinly sliced
2 tablespoons sea salt
¼ teaspoon celery seeds
1 teaspoon mustard seeds
2 tablespoons prepared horseradish
5 whole cloves
250 ml/1 cup white wine vinegar
200 g/1 cup granulated sugar

SERVES 6–8

To make the pickles, put the cucumbers, onion and salt in a large non-metal bowl. Cover and chill in the fridge for 2 hours. Rinse and drain well. Transfer to a medium container. In a small saucepan, heat the celery seeds, mustard seeds, horseradish, cloves, vinegar and sugar. Bring to the boil, to dissolve the sugar, then pour into the container with the cucumbers. Cover and refrigerate for 1 day to develop a full flavour.

To make the gravadlax, pound the juniper berries, fennel seeds, peppercorns, 1 tablespoon of the salt and the sugar with a pestle and mortar until roughly crushed and aromatic.

Line a non-metal tray with clingfilm/plastic wrap, leaving enough overlapping to wrap around the salmon later. Scatter one-quarter of the ground spices over the clingfilm/plastic wrap and lay the salmon, skin-side down, on top. Cover with the rest of the ground spices. Wrap tightly in the clingfilm/plastic wrap so you form a watertight parcel and weight down with cans of food or a heavy board. Leave to cure for 12 hours or overnight in the fridge. Flip the fish over, weight down again and cure for another 12 hours and continue to cure and flip until the fish has had 48 hours.

Unwrap the fish and drain off any juices. Place on a board, skin-side down. Slice the gravadlax thinly with a sharp knife, cutting the flesh away from the skin (discard the skin). Serve with buttered rye bread and the pickles.

Spaghetti & Meatballs

IF THERE'S ONE THING TONY SOPRANO LIKES MORE THAN INTIMIDATING PEOPLE, CHEATING ON HIS WIFE AND SNIFFING OUT A 'RAT', IT'S ITALIAN FOOD. THESE MAFIA MEATBALLS WITH SPAGHETTI 'JUST LIKE MAMA USED TO MAKE' WILL PROVIDE MUCH GRATIFICATION AS YOU OBSERVE THE GANGSTER GOINGS-ON IN *THE SOPRANOS*.

500 g/1 lb. 2 oz. spaghetti
salt
freshly grated Parmesan cheese,
   to serve

SPAGHETTI SAUCE
90 g/¾ cup chopped onion
6 cloves garlic, minced
50 g/3½ tablespoons extra-virgin
   olive oil
2 x 400-g/14-oz. cans whole,
   peeled tomatoes
2 teaspoons sea salt
1 teaspoon granulated sugar
1 fresh bay leaf
170 g/6 oz. tomato purée/paste
¾ teaspoon dried basil
½ teaspoon ground black pepper

MEATBALLS
2 tablespoons extra-virgin olive
   oil
225 g/½ lb. lean minced/ground
   beef
225 g/½ lb ground thin/short rib
1 cup fresh bread crumbs
1 tablespoons dried parsley
2 tablespoons freshly grated
   Parmesan cheese
¼ teaspoon ground black pepper
a pinch of garlic powder
1 egg, beaten

SERVES 4

For the spaghetti sauce, in a large saucepan over a medium heat, sauté the onion and garlic in the olive oil until the onion is translucent. Stir in the tomatoes, salt, sugar and bay leaf. Cover the saucepan and reduce the heat to low. Simmer for 1–1½ hours. Stir in the tomato purée/paste, basil and black pepper.

Preheat the oven to 190°C (375°F) Gas 5.

Combine all the ingredients for the meatballs in a mixing bowl with your hands and form into golf ball-size balls. Place on a baking sheet and transfer to the preheated oven for 20 minutes.

Bring a pot of salted water to a boil and add the pasta. When the pasta reaches an al dente texture, about 8–10 minutes, remove and drain. Mix with the sauce, add the meatballs and finish by adding a generous sprinkling of freshly grated Parmesan cheese.

To make in a slow-cooker, set the heat to its lowest setting and cook the meatballs and sauce for 6–8 hours. Follow the above directions for cooking pasta.

St Clement's Cakes

THESE CITRUSY CAKES ARE SO ARRESTINGLY GOOD THAT YOU'LL WANT TO SMUGGLE AS MANY AS YOU CAN ONTO YOUR PLATE AS YOU BINGE-WATCH *ORANGE IS THE NEW BLACK*. THEY'RE CERTAINLY MORE APPETIZING THAN ANYTHING RED WOULD SERVE UP.

finely grated zest and freshly squeezed juice of 1 large orange

finely grated zest and freshly squeezed juice of 1 large lemon

55 g/¼ cup orange marmalade

35 g/¼ cup finely chopped mixed candied peel

2 teaspoons orange liqueur, such as Cointreau or Grand Marnier

160 g/1½ sticks butter, softened

160 g/¾ cup caster/granulated sugar

3 eggs, lightly beaten

40 g/3 tablespoons ground almonds

120 g/1 cup plain/all-purpose flour

50 g/⅓ cup self-raising/self-rising flour

CANDIED CITRUS SLICES

200 g/1 cup caster/granulated sugar

20 g/4 teaspoons glucose syrup/ liquid glucose

1 orange, sliced 7 mm/⅓ inch thick

1 lemon, sliced 7 mm/⅓ inch thick

8 small panettone cases

SERVES 8–10

To make the Candied Citrus Slices, put the sugar, glucose and 40 ml/ 2½ tablespoons water in a large, stainless steel saucepan and slowly bring to the boil – do not stir. Remove from the heat and, using metal tongs, place the fruit in the mixture, ensuring the pieces do not overlap. Over a low heat, boil the fruit for about 15 minutes, turning 4 times to ensure even cooking. Let cool in the syrup, then shake off any excess syrup and let dry on waxed paper.

Preheat the oven to 170°C (325°F) Gas 3.

Put the citrus zest and juice, marmalade, mixed peel and liqueur in a bowl, stir and let soak. Meanwhile, cream the butter and sugar together in a large bowl until pale and fluffy. Add the beaten eggs in 2 stages, stirring to a smooth batter each time. With a wooden spoon, fold in the ground almonds and both flours, stirring until smooth. Add the soaked fruit mixture and stir until evenly distributed. Spoon the mixture into the panettone cases and smooth level with a palette knife or metal spatula.

Bake in the preheated oven for 35 minutes. Remove the cakes from the oven and place a candied citrus slice on each cake. Return to oven for a further 5–10 minutes. A skewer inserted in the middle of the cakes should come out clean. If they appear to be colouring too quickly, cover with baking parchment. Let cool on a wire rack. They will keep in an airtight container for 3–4 days, or can be frozen for up to 2 months.

Variation

To make 1 large cake, make the mixture as above, then spoon into a lined, 18-cm/ 7-inch round cake pan and bake for 40 minutes. Remove from the oven, place the candied citrus slices on top, then return to the oven for 15–20 minutes.

"HERE COME THE MEAT SWEATS."
— JOEY TRIBBIANI, *FRIENDS*

Chapter 5

FEATURED SHOWS
*Friends, Frasier, Cheers, The Marvellous Mrs Maisel,
The Good Place, Parks & Recreation.*

OTHER SHOWS
*It's Always Sunny in Philadelphia, Family Guy, How I Met Your Mother,
The Big Bang Theory, Modern Family, Arrested Development,
The Office, The Simpsons, Will & Grace, Curb Your Enthusiasm,
30 Rock, The Fresh Prince of Bel Air.*

Just For Laughs

GIGGLESOME GRUB

FRASIER MAY NOT KNOW WHAT TO DO WITH THOSE TOSSED SALADS
AND SCRAMBLED EGGS, BUT THE ANSWER SHOULD BE SIMPLE ENOUGH.
EAT THEM! FOOD CAN BE A LOT OF THINGS: TASTY, FILLING, INTRIGUING,
IMPRESSIVE... BUT FUNNY? WELL, YES. WHETHER IT'S TOM IN *Parks &
Recreation* EXPLAINING THAT HE CALLS SANDWICHES 'ADAM SANDLERS',
NOODLES 'LONG-ASS RICE' AND EGGS 'PRE-BIRDS OR FUTURE BIRDS';
CHANDLER IN *Friends* DEADPANNING THAT HE FINDS MONICA'S AMUSE-
BOUCHE TO BE 'AMUSE-ING'; OR THE ENTIRE CAST OF *Cheers* FLINGING
THEIR THANKSGIVING DINNER AT EACH OTHER IN AN ALMIGHTY FOOD
FIGHT, FOOD CAN BE GOSH-DARN HILARIOUS. WHEN IT COMES TO
LAUGHABLE LIBATIONS, COMICAL CUISINE AND FUNNY FARE, THIS MIRTHFUL
MENU IS WHERE IT'S AT. SO, WHILE YOU'RE BELLY-LAUGHING, YOU CAN
ALSO BE BELLY-FILLING WITH THESE TICKLE-MY-TASTEBUDS TREATS.

Trifle Cheesecakes

IT'S GUARANTEED THAT THESE MINI TRIFLES WILL TASTE 1,000 TIMES BETTER THAN THE ONE RACHEL ATTEMPTS IN *FRIENDS*. IT MAY SEEM LIKE A TRIFLING MATTER BUT IT'S WORTH REASSURING YOU THAT THEY WON'T TASTE LIKE FEET AND THERE'S NO HIDDEN BEEF SAUTÉED WITH PEAS AND ONIONS – PHEW!

1 small raspberry jam Swiss roll/ jelly roll
200 g/1½ cups fresh raspberries
3 tablespoons amaretto or almond liqueur
65 g/2½ oz. raspberry jelly cubes/jello powder
250 g/generous 1 cup mascarpone cheese
250 ml/1 cup sour cream
2 tablespoons icing/ confectioners' sugar, or to taste
1 teaspoon vanilla bean paste
sugar sprinkles, to decorate

6 small Kilner jars or jam jars with lids
a piping/pastry bag fitted with a large round nozzle/tip

SERVES 6

Cut the Swiss roll/jelly roll into thin slices, then cut each slice in half. Arrange the slices around the sides of each jar and a slice in the base. Sprinkle over the raspberries and drizzle with the amaretto.

Make up the raspberry jelly/jello according to the package instructions and pour it into the jars, dividing it equally between them. Leave to set in the refrigerator.

Once the jelly/jello has set, prepare the cheesecake topping. In a large mixing bowl, whisk together the mascarpone and sour cream until smooth. Sift the icing/confectioners' sugar over the mixture, add the vanilla paste, and fold through, testing for sweetness and adding a little more icing/confectioners' sugar if you prefer.

Spoon the cheese mixture into the piping/pastry bag and pipe blobs on top of each trifle, making sure that the jelly/jello is covered completely. Decorate with sugar sprinkles to serve.

Orange Crush Cookies

ENJOY THESE ZESTY TREATS WITH A SIDE OF COFFEE AS YOU WITNESS FRASIER AND NILES SHOOT THE BREEZE AT CAFE NERVOSA FOR AN ENTIRE EPISODE OF *FRASIER*. TOPICS COVERED INCLUDE: NILES'S SEXUALITY, HIS ILLICIT DESIRE FOR DAPHNE, THEIR DAD AND, ER, HAND CREAM.

120 g/1 stick butter, at room temperature, chopped
100 g/½ cup caster/granulated sugar
40 g/3½ tablespoons muscovado or soft brown sugar
2 teaspoons pure vanilla extract
1 drop of orange extract or orange flower water
2 teaspoons single/light cream
1 egg
180 g/1⅓ cups plain/all-purpose flour, plus extra for dusting
1 teaspoon unsweetened cocoa powder
½ teaspoon baking powder
¼ teaspoon salt
85 g/½ cup dark/semi-sweet chocolate chips
finely grated zest of ½ orange

2 baking sheets, lined with non-stick baking paper

MAKES ABOUT 25

Put the butter in a bowl and beat with a wooden spoon until very soft. Beat in the sugars until well incorporated and creamy, then add the vanilla extract, orange extract or flower water, cream and egg, and beat in. Gradually sift in the flour, cocoa powder, baking powder and salt, and mix until combined. Finally, mix in the chocolate chips and orange zest. Cover and refrigerate for 30 minutes.

Preheat the oven to 170°C (325°F) Gas 3.

Remove the bowl from the fridge. Lightly flour a clean work surface and roll the chilled dough into a sausage roughly 30 cm/12 inches long. Cut the dough into about 25 equal slices and arrange on the prepared baking sheets.

Bake in the preheated oven for about 15–20 minutes until browned. Allow the cookies to cool on the baking sheets for 5 minutes, then transfer to a wire rack to finish cooling.

Matchstick Fries
with Sichuan Pepper Salt

PREPARE THESE BAR SNACKS AS YOU SETTLE DOWN TO WATCH *CHEERS*, THE TAVERN WHERE EVERYBODY KNOWS YOUR NAME. IMAGINE YOU'RE SITTING AT THE END OF THE BAR IN-BETWEEN NORM AND CLIFF, MUNCHING ON THESE MATCHSTICK FRIES, SIPPING A BEER AND MOCKING THE DIM-BUT-DELIGHTFUL WOODY.

2 large floury potatoes, roughly the same size
cornflour/cornstarch, for dusting
vegetable or sunflower oil, for deep-frying

SICHUAN PEPPER SALT
1 tablespoon Sichuan peppercorns
2 tablespoons coarse rock salt

SERVES 4

For the Sichuan Pepper Salt, heat the peppercorns in a small frying pan/skillet until hot but not smoking. Transfer to a plate to cool. Combine with the salt and grind in a spice mill or with a pestle and mortar. Set aside.

Peel the potatoes and trim on all sides to get a block. Cut the block into thin slices, then cut the slices thinly into matchsticks.

Put the potatoes into a bowl of iced water for at least 5 minutes to remove excess starch and prevent sticking when frying. Put some cornflour/cornstarch in a shallow bowl.

Fill a large saucepan one-third full with oil or, if using a deep-fryer, follow the manufacturer's instructions. Heat the oil to 190°C (375°F) or until a cube of bread browns in 30 seconds.

Drain the potatoes and dry very well, then toss to coat lightly with the cornflour/cornstarch. Put in a sieve/strainer to help shake off any excess cornflour/cornstarch.

Working in batches, fry about a handful of potatoes at a time. Place the potatoes in a frying basket and lower into the hot oil carefully. Fry for about 5 minutes. Remove and drain on paper towels. Repeat until all of the potatoes have been fried.

Sprinkle with the Sichuan Pepper Salt and serve.

Pastrami Reuben on Rye
with Russian Dressing

HANG WITH MIDGE AND HER STRAIGHT-TALKING MANAGER SUSIE AT THE STAGE DELI IN *THE MARVELLOUS MRS MAISEL*, WHERE THE PASTRAMI REUBENS ON RYE ARE PLENTIFUL, THE STUFFED CABBAGE IS ABUNDANT, AND THE LAUGHS JUST KEEP ON COMING.

225 g/1⅓ cup sauerkraut, drained and squeezed of moisture
8 slices rye bread
butter, softened, for spreading
8–16 slices Provolone cheese
450 g/1 lb. pastrami, shaved
sea salt and freshly ground black pepper
fries, to serve

RUSSIAN DRESSING
340 g/1½ cups mayonnaise
150 ml/⅔ cup chilli/chile sauce
75 g/⅓ cup sour cream
2 tablespoons horseradish sauce
1 tablespoon freshly squeezed lemon juice
2 teaspoons sugar
2 teaspoons Worcestershire sauce
½ teaspoon hot sauce
½ teaspoon paprika
1 dill pickle, chopped
1 spring onion/scallion, chopped

MAKES 4

To make the Russian Dressing, mix all the ingredients in a food processor until combined. Season with salt and pepper to taste, and refrigerate until needed.

Build the sandwich: mix half of the Russian Dressing with the sauerkraut. Butter all 8 slices of rye bread. Arrange 4 of the slices butter-side down and place 1–2 slices of Provolone cheese on each one, followed by a generous serving of pastrami and another 1–2 slices of cheese. Top with the sauerkraut mixture and a second piece of bread, butter-side up.

Heat a griddle/grill pan over a low-medium heat. Add the sandwiches and cook for about 2–3 minutes per side, until the cheese has melted. Serve with fries and extra Russian Dressing on the side.

Grilled Shrimp with Green Salsa

IT'S NOT ADVISABLE TO STUFF THESE BAD BOYS INTO YOUR BRA – À LA ELEANOR IN *THE GOOD PLACE* – BUT THEY TASTE SO HEAVENLY, YOU'LL PROBABLY WANT TO STUFF YOUR FACE WITH THEM. WHAT THE HELL!

2 tomatoes
1 tablespoon very finely chopped onion
1 green chilli/chile
1 small bunch of coriander/cilantro, finely chopped
¼ teaspoon sea salt
15 g/1½ tablespoons butter
6 large prawns/shrimp, shell on
5 garlic cloves, very finely chopped

SERVES 2

Put the tomatoes, onion, chilli/chile and 500 ml/2 cups water in a saucepan over a high heat. Cover with a lid and bring to the boil, then turn the heat down to low and simmer for about 5–7 minutes.

Drain, then allow to cool for at least 5 minutes before transferring to a food processor with the coriander/cilantro and half the salt. Whizz for 2 minutes and set aside.

Heat a stovetop griddle/grill pan or frying pan/skillet over a medium heat.

Put the butter and prawns/shrimp in the pan and cook for about 3–4 minutes or until opaque and cooked through, turning occasionally. Add the garlic and cook for 2 minutes.

Divide the prawns/shrimp between 2 dishes and spoon some of the coriander/cilantro sauce over them. Serve with the remaining sauce on the side for dipping.

Garbage Cookies

JOIN LESLIE AND APRIL IN *PARKS & RECREATION* AS THEY BECOME GARBAGE COLLECTORS FOR THE DAY IN A BID TO BRING GENDER EQUALITY TO THEIR GOVERNMENT. AFTER A TOUGH DAY TALKING TRASH, THEY COULD'VE DONE WITH A BATCH OF THESE DUMPSTER-LICIOUS COOKIES.

100 g/7 tablespoons unsalted butter
100 g/½ cup light brown sugar
125 g/⅔ cup caster/granulated sugar
1 UK large/US extra-large egg plus 1 UK large/US extra-large egg yolk
200 g/1½ cups self-raising/self-rising flour
40 g/½ cup porridge oats
20 g/1 cup puffed rice cereal (such as Rice Krispies)
100 g/⅔ cup M&M's
30 g/1 cup pretzels, crushed
30 g/1 cup lightly salted potato chips, crushed
65 g/½ cup dark/bittersweet chocolate chips
50 g/⅓ cup white chocolate chips

3 baking sheets lined with non-stick baking paper

MAKES 18

Preheat the oven to 180°C (350°F) Gas 4.

Cream together the butter and both sugars in the bowl of a free-standing mixer or in a large mixing bowl with a hand-held electric whisk. Add in the egg and egg yolk, and mix until fully combined. Gradually add in the flour until you have a sticky cookie dough. Fold in the oats and Rice Krispies by hand.

Add in the M&M's, crushed pretzels, crushed potato chips and both chocolate chips. Use your hands to bring the dough together and make sure all of the additions are evenly distributed throughout.

Use an ice cream scoop to portion the cookies, then roll them in your hands, before flattening them slightly and spacing well apart on the lined baking sheets.

Bake the cookies in the preheated oven for 8–10 minutes until light golden brown on the edges.

Leave the cookies to cool for 2 minutes on the baking sheets before carefully removing them and transferring them to a wire rack to cool completely. Wait until they are completely cool before eating.

Note
These cookies are best eaten once they are cool, on the day they are made, but can be stored for up to 3 days in an airtight container at room temperature.

"I'M NOT RISKING MY HEALTH EATING TRASH-FOOD.
I MEAN, UNLESS IT'S A CORN DOG."
– TURK, *SCRUBS*

Chapter 6

FEATURED SHOWS
*House, Grey's Anatomy, ER, Nurse Jackie,
Nip/Tuck, Scrubs.*

OTHER SHOWS
*The Good Doctor, The Resident, Call the Midwife, Chicago Med,
New Amsterdam, Casualty, Holby City, Code Black, The Night Shift,
Saving Hope, Dr. Quinn Medicine Woman, Chicago Hope,
The Knick, Doctors.*

Doctors & Nurses

MEDICAL MUNCHIES

WHETHER YOU'RE TEAM MCDREAMY OR TEAM MCSTEAMY, CHANCES ARE
YOU'LL NEED TO DO SOME SERIOUS COMFORT-EATING WHEN INDULGING
IN A MEDICAL DRAMA. THE HIGHS, THE LOWS, THE DEATHS, THE INFIDELITIES,
THE LIES, THE ADDICTIONS... IT'S NOT JUST THE PATIENTS WHO NEED A LIE
DOWN. THE SHEER EMOTION OF IT ALL WILL HAVE YOU REACHING FOR
THE TISSUES IN-BETWEEN EACH BITE OF WHATEVER'S ON YOUR PLATE. BUT
IT'S NOT ALL TEARS, TANTRUMS, TABLETS AND TRAUMA – THE MEDICAL GENRE
CAN ALSO MAKE FUN OF ITSELF, WITH SHOWS LIKE *Scrubs* AND 'CUTTING-
EDGE' RIDICULOUSNESS WITH CHRISTIAN'S AND SEAN'S ANTICS IN *Nip/Tuck*.
NEVER HAS THE PHRASE 'TRUST ME, I'M A DOCTOR' BEEN MORE MISGUIDED.
SO, WHETHER YOU'LL BE SOBBING INTO YOUR SMOOTHIE OR CHORTLING
INTO YOUR COOKIES, YOU'RE SURE TO BE BLUE-LIGHTED TO YUMMYVILLE
WITH THE FOLLOWING RECIPES.

Coffee Addict's Brownies

PLAY *HOUSE* WITH THESE CAFFEINE-LADEN BROWNIES AS YOU WATCH DR. HOUSE MAINLINE PAIN PILLS, IRK HIS COLLEAGUES AND POUR BREWS FROM THE COFFEE MACHINE THAT STATES: 'GOOD COFFEE CHEAPER THAN PROZAC'. HOUSE BY THE WAY, HISTORY-OF-USE, WHO KNEW?

225 g/8 oz. dark/bittersweet chocolate (55% cocoa), chopped
200 g/1¾ sticks butter, chopped
4 eggs
130 g/⅔ cup caster/granulated sugar
125 g/1 scant cup plain/all-purpose flour
1½ tablespoons instant coffee or espresso granules

20-cm/8-inch square baking pan, greased and dusted with flour

MAKES 6–8

Preheat the oven to 170°C (325°F) Gas 3.

Put the chocolate and butter in a heatproof bowl set over a saucepan of barely simmering water. Do not let the base of the bowl touch the water. Allow to melt, stirring occasionally, until completely smooth. Remove from the heat.

In a separate bowl, whisk the eggs and sugar for 1–2 minutes. Sift in the flour, add the coffee and whisk again to mix. Pour the chocolate mixture in and mix well with a wooden spoon.

Spoon the mixture into the prepared baking pan, spread level with a spatula and bake in the preheated oven for about 25 minutes. Allow the brownies to cool in the pan for a few minutes, then turn out onto a wire rack to cool completely.

Serve at room temperature, cut into equal portions.

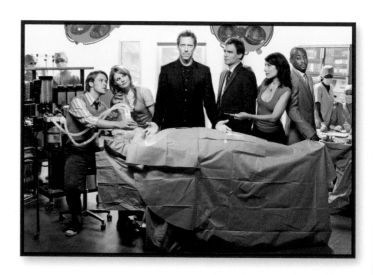

Blueberry Muffins

BAKING CAN BE VERY THERAPEUTIC – AT LEAST, IT IS FOR IZZIE IN *GREY'S ANATOMY*. GRAB YOUR WOODEN SPOON AND JOIN HER IN HER GRIEF-STRICKEN MUFFIN-BAKING SPREE [SPOILER ALERT] AFTER DENNY DIES.

250 ml/1 cup buttermilk
100 g/7 tablespoons unsalted butter, melted and cooled slightly
1 UK large/US extra-large egg, beaten
250 g/2 cups plain/all-purpose flour
1 teaspoon baking powder
1 teaspoon bicarbonate of soda/baking soda
200 g/1 cup caster/granulated sugar
a pinch of salt
200 g/1⅓ cups fresh blueberries

a 12-hole muffin pan, lined with paper cases

MAKES 12

Whisk together the buttermilk, melted butter and egg in a large glass measuring jug/pitcher. Sift together the flour, baking powder and bicarbonate of soda/baking soda in a large mixing bowl and add the sugar and salt. Pour the wet ingredients into the dry and use a fork to combine gently. Leave the batter to rest for at least 1 hour or in the fridge overnight.

Preheat the oven to 200°C (400°F) Gas 6.

Fold in the blueberries, divide the batter among the paper cases and bake for 20–25 minutes. Leave to cool slightly before tucking in.

Meatball Deep-Dish Pizza

SET IN CHICAGO – WHICH IS FAMOUS FOR ITS DEEP-DISH PIZZA – THE 15 SEASONS OF *ER* WILL TAKE YOU ON A ROLLERCOASTER RIDE OF RESUSCITATIONS, ROMANTIC ENTANGLEMENTS AND RANDOM ACTS OF REBELLION. DEVOUR THEM ALL ALONG WITH THIS DISH.

450 g/1 lb. beef meatballs
300 g/10½ oz. fresh mozzarella, patted dry and torn into pieces
3 tablespoons grated Parmesan

DOUGH
¼ tablespoon active dried yeast
¼ tablespoon sugar
60 g/¼ cup clarified butter or shortening
260 g/2 cups plain/all-purpose flour
salt

SAUCE
1 onion, finely chopped
2 tablespoons olive oil
2 garlic cloves, thinly sliced
400-g/14-oz. can tomatoes
1 pear, peeled, cored and chopped into small pieces
1 heaped teaspoon dried oregano
1 bay leaf

a non-stick 20-cm/8-inch loose-bottomed cake pan

SERVES 2

For the dough, mix 175 ml/¾ cup water with the yeast and sugar and leave for 5 minutes. Put the yeast mixture, butter or shortening, 130 g/1 cup flour and a pinch of salt in an electric mixer with a dough hook and mix for 5 minutes. Add 100 g/¾ cup more flour and mix until a dough forms. Add the remaining flour if needed. The dough should be wet, but shouldn't stick to your hands. Put the dough in a covered bowl in the fridge to rise overnight. Remove 2–3 hours before use.

To make the sauce, lightly sauté the onion in a heavy-based casserole dish with the olive oil and garlic. When the onion is translucent and soft, add the tomatoes, pear pieces, oregano and bay leaf. Cook slowly for 1 hour, stirring occasionally, until the pear has dissolved into the tomatoes. Remove the bay leaf. Blitz with a stick blender until smooth.

Preheat the oven to its highest setting. Brown the meatballs in a frying pan/skillet and add them to the tomato sauce. Pat out the dough in the cake pan, and up the sides. Make sure you pat the dough firmly all around the edge using your knuckles. Place three-quarters of the mozzarella in the bottom of the pan. Cover with the meatballs and tomato. Top with the remaining mozzarella and the Parmesan. Bake for about 25–30 minutes until the crust is puffed and golden. If the inside is still soupy, return to the oven for another 5–10 minutes.

To serve, remove the sides of the cake pan and cut the pizza into slices.

Devil's Food Cake

IS *NURSE JACKIE* A SAINT OR A SINNER? WHILE YOU'RE PONDERING THIS, DELIGHT IN THIS DEVILISHLY DELICIOUS CHOCOLATE CAKE THAT THOR WOULD DEFINITELY APPROVE OF: "I DON'T DRINK. I DON'T SMOKE. I EAT CAKE. IT'S COMFORT FOOD," HE SAYS.

250 g/2 sticks butter
250 ml/1 cup full-fat/whole milk
125 g/⅔ cup dark muscovado sugar
175 g/generous ¾ cup caster/ granulated sugar
3 eggs
150 g/generous 1 cup plain/ all-purpose flour
125 g/1 cup unsweetened cocoa powder
1 teaspoon bicarbonate of soda/ baking soda
½ teaspoon baking powder
¼ teaspoon salt
4 fresh red chillies/chiles, deseeded and finely chopped

DEVIL HORNS
200 g/1 cup caster/granulated sugar
2 long red fresh chillies/chiles

CHOCOLATE FUDGE FROSTING
350 g/12 oz. dark/bittersweet chocolate, chopped
225 g/8 oz. unsalted butter
225 ml/scant 1 cup full-fat/whole milk
1 teaspoon pure vanilla extract
450 g/3¼ cups icing/ confectioner's sugar, sifted
1–2 teaspoons chilli/chile syrup (reserved from Devil Horns)

2 x 20-cm/8-inch cake pans, greased and lined with non-stick baking paper

SERVES 12–16

First, make the devil horns. Put the sugar and 200 ml/¾ cup water in a saucepan set over a gentle heat and stir until the sugar has fully dissolved. Increase the heat and boil for 1 minute. Prick the stalk end of the chillies/chiles with a skewer. Reduce the heat, add the chillies/chiles and simmer gently for 40 minutes, or until they have begun to turn translucent and the sugar has slightly thickened. Turn off the heat and leave them to cool in their syrup overnight. Reserve the syrup.

Preheat the oven to 180°C (350°F) Gas 4.

Put the butter, milk and dark muscovado sugar in a saucepan and stir over a gentle heat until the sugar and butter have melted. Whisk together the caster/granulated sugar and eggs in a large mixing bowl until light and fluffy. Continue to whisk, while gradually adding the hot butter mixture. Sift over the flour, cocoa powder, bicarbonate of soda/baking soda, baking powder and salt, and whisk until fully combined.

Fold in the chopped chillies/chiles and divide the batter between the two prepared pans and bake for 25–30 minutes or until an inserted skewer comes out clean. Leave the cakes to cool in their pans on a wire rack for 10 minutes before turning out onto the wire rack to cool completely.

For the frosting, put the chocolate and butter in a heatproof bowl set over a pan of simmering water. Stir until smooth and combined. Set aside to cool slightly. In a separate bowl, whisk together the milk, vanilla and icing/ confectioner's sugar. Stir in the cooled chocolate mixture. Add the chilli/ chile syrup and whisk until spreadable. Sandwich the cakes together with half the frosting and spread the rest over the top and sides. Place the devil horns on top of the cake.

Green Giant & Apple Zinger

THE PLASTIC-SURGEON BEST FRIENDS IN *NIP/TUCK* DRINK WHEATGRASS SMOOTHIES. PRESUMABLY IT GIVES THEM THE ENERGY TO PERFORM COUNTLESS BOOB JOBS, DISPOSE OF CORPSES, AND ENGAGE IN SOME PRETTY KINKY SHENANIGANS. CLEARLY THESE GREEN GLASSFULS ARE A CUT ABOVE!

GREEN GIANT
1 chilled cucumber, quartered
   lengthways
3 handfuls of watercress
1 head of broccoli, both florets
   and stalks, chopped
freshly squeezed juice of
   ½ lemon
½ teaspoon extra-virgin olive oil
1–2 teaspoons wheatgrass
   powder

SERVES 2

APPLE ZINGER
4 apples, quartered, cored and
   cut into wedges
2.5-cm/1-inch piece of fresh root
   ginger, unpeeled
2 large handfuls of fresh spinach
1 teaspoon freshly squeezed
   lemon juice
1 teaspoon powdered greens
1 teaspoon wheatgrass powder

SERVES 2

Green Giant
Juice the cucumber, watercress (if your machine struggles with the watercress, add a splash of water or some of the lemon juice), broccoli florets and stalks. Stir in the lemon juice, olive oil and wheatgrass. Chill and serve in a tall glass.

Apple Zinger
Juice the apples, ginger and spinach then stir in the lemon juice, powdered greens and wheatgrass. Chill and serve in a tall glass.

Peanut Butter Cookies

YOU'LL MOST CERTAINLY NEED A PAIR OF COOKIE PANTS LIKE ELLIOT'S IN *SCRUBS* WHEN YOU BAKE THESE CHEWY YET CRUNCHY CHOMPS. CHANNEL J.D. AND GOBBLE THEM IN ONE GO BEFORE ANYONE – LIKE TURK – HAS A CHANCE TO SWIPE THEM.

300 g/1¼ cups unsweetened crunchy peanut butter
1–2 tablespoons soft brown sugar
a pinch of salt
2 eggs, beaten
50 g/⅓ cup roasted and salted peanuts, crushed

a baking sheet lined with non-stick baking paper

MAKES ABOUT 10

Preheat the oven to 180°C (350°F) Gas 4.

Put the peanut butter into a large mixing bowl and stir in the sugar and salt. Add all but a tablespoon of the beaten eggs and mix together thoroughly.

Form the mixture into balls the size of walnuts and arrange on the prepared baking sheet, leaving a little space for spreading between each one. Press down gently with the tines of a fork to flatten the cookies slightly.

Bake in the preheated oven for 12–15 minutes, until the cookies are firm and golden.

Transfer to a wire rack to cool, store in an airtight container or cookie jar and eat within 1 week.

"DON'T DRINK AND DRIVE. BUT IF YOU DO, CALL ME."
– JIMMY MCGILL, *BETTER CALL SAUL*

Chapter 7

FEATURED SHOWS
The Good Wife, Suits, Ally McBeal,
Law & Order, Better Call Saul.

OTHER SHOWS
L.A. Law, The People vs. O.J. Simpson, Boston Legal,
The Practice, Chicago Justice, Judging Amy, Raising the Bar,
The Firm, Eli Stone, Judge John Deed, The Jury, Shark,
Fairly Legal, For the People, Goliath, Damages.

Legal Eagles

ORDER! ORDER!

FOOD AND TV SHOWS ABOUT THE LAW DON'T MIX. OBJECTION,
YOUR HONOUR! THEY MOST CERTAINLY DO. AND TO PROVE IT,
CHECK OUT THIS COLLECTION OF DISHES SO APPETIZING THAT EVEN
LADY JUSTICE HERSELF WOULD REMOVE HER BLINDFOLD, PUT DOWN
HER SWORD AND SET OF SCALES, AND GET STUCK IN. AS FOR THE
COCKTAIL RECIPES? WELL, IT'S NOT SO MUCH A CASE OF LAW AND
ORDER AS IT IS POUR AND ORDER (ME ANOTHER ONE). THE EVIDENCE
SUGGESTS THAT YOU'LL BE SMACKING YOUR LIPS AND SWINGING YOUR
HIPS ALONG WITH *Ally McBeal*'S IMAGINARY DANCING BABY... BUT,
ULTIMATELY, YOU'LL HAVE TO BE THE JUDGE. AS FOR HOW MUCH
HARVEY SPECTER IN *Suits* MUST HAVE SPENT ON WHISKEY DURING
HIS TIME AS A LAWYER? THE JURY'S STILL OUT.

Smoking President

IT'S LITTLE WONDER ALICIA KNOCKS BACK TEQUILA AFTER TEQUILA IN *THE GOOD WIFE*. WOULDN'T YOU IF YOUR HUSBAND WAS PHOTOGRAPHED SMOKING CRACK WITH A PROSTITUTE, THEN LATER DECIDED TO RUN FOR PRESIDENT? A SMOKING PRESIDENT, INDEED? TSK!

60 ml/2 fl oz. Los Danzantes Reposado Mezcal
5 ml/1 teaspoon agave nectar
2 drops of Bob's lavender bitters
2 drops of Bob's cardamom bitters
ice cubes
lemon zest twist and fresh lavender sprig, to garnish

MAKES 1

Stir all the drink ingredients over cubed ice in a rocks glass for 30–40 seconds, or until the desired level of dilution is reached. Gently squeeze the lemon zest garnish to express the citrus oils into the glass. Garnish the glass with the lemon zest and a lavender sprig.

Hot Dogs with Remoulade Sauce

DURING ITS 20-SEASON RUN, IN-BETWEEN ALL THE CRIME-SOLVING, JUSTICE-SEEKING AND MELODRAMA, THE CHARACTERS ON *LAW & ORDER* CAN BE SEEN CHOWING DOWN ON MANY A HOT DOG. ORDER! ORDER! (YOURS NOW).

350 ml/1½ cups beer (any lager will do)
6 pork or beef frankfurters
6 long white, fluffy hot-dog buns
6 tablespoons diced shallot
4 tablespoons sweet hot-dog mustard (or use 3 tablespoons Dijon mustard mixed with 2 tablespoons brown sugar and 1 teaspoon hot water)
4 tablespoons ketchup
6 tablespoons store-bought crispy fried onions

REMOULADE SAUCE
1 egg yolk
1 teaspoon Dijon mustard
180 ml/¾ cup neutral-tasting oil
1 tablespoon white wine vinegar
2 teaspoons chopped gherkins
2 teaspoons chopped capers
1 tablespoon chopped chervil

MAKES 6

Pour the beer into a large saucepan and heat until simmering. Braise the frankfurters in the beer until they are hot. Remove from the beer with metal tongs and put on paper towels to drain.

Split the buns down the middle and lightly toast them. Add one braised sausage and some diced raw shallot to each bun.

Add about a tablespoon each of mustard, Remoulade Sauce and tomato ketchup in a stripe down each sausage. Top with the crispy fried onions and eat whilst still hot.

Cherry Pavlova

THE ATTENTION-SEEKING ELAINE IN *ALLY MCBEAL* IS NOTHING IF NOT IMAGINATIVE. DIVE INTO THIS EPIC MERINGUE WHILE YOU MARVEL AT HER MADCAP INVENTIONS – FROM THE FACE BRA TO CUSTOMIZED CONDOMS, THE TOILET SEAT WARMER TO HER EDIBLE CHERRY-FLAVOURED UNDERWEAR.

4 egg whites
250 g/1¼ cups caster/superfine sugar

TOPPING
250 ml/1 cup whipping cream
400-g/14-oz. can black cherries, or fresh cherries, stoned/pitted

SERVES 6

Preheat the oven to 150°C/300°F/Gas 2.

Using a pencil, mark out the circumference of a dinner plate on a sheet of baking paper. Place it on a baking sheet, pencil marking-side down.

Whisk the egg whites with an electric mixer until they form stiff peaks, then whisk in the sugar, 1 tablespoon at a time, until the meringue looks glossy and thick.

Spread the meringue inside the circle, creating a crater by making the sides a little higher than the middle. Bake for 1–1½ hours, then turn off the heat and let the pavlova cool completely inside the oven. This is important, otherwise it will be soggy, not gooey.

Just before serving, whip the cream into soft peaks and gently spread over the meringue, piling it into the centre and spreading it outwards. Then pile on the cherries. If you are using canned ones, you will have to drain them first (but keep all that delicious syrup – and serve it in a jug/pitcher alongside the pavlova).

Whiskey Sour

EXPENSIVE WHISKEY FEATURES HEAVILY IN HARVEY SPECTER'S LIFE. AS DO EXPENSIVE *SUITS*.
WHETHER HE'S DRINKING AND CHATTING (WITH MIKE), DRINKING AND FLIRTING (WITH DONNA),
OR DRINKING AND CRYING (AT HIS DAD'S GRAVESIDE), JOIN HIM ON THE WHISKEY WAGON
WITH YOUR OWN CLASSY COCKTAIL.

**50 ml/2 fl. oz. Woodford Reserve
Bourbon**
**25 ml/1 fl. oz. freshly squeezed
lemon juice**
25 ml/1 fl. oz. simple sugar syrup
20 ml/⅔ fl. oz. egg white
**3 dashes Angostura bitters, plus
extra to serve**
ice cubes
**lemon slice and Luxardo
maraschino cherry, to garnish**

MAKES I

Combine all the drink ingredients in a cocktail shaker and 'dry'
shake first with no ice to emulsify the egg white. Add a scoop of
cubed ice and shake vigorously.

Strain into a rocks glass over some cubed ice and garnish with
a lemon slice, Luxardo maraschino cherry and an extra dash of
Angostura bitters.

Cinnamon Buns

AFTER FLEEING AND CHANGING HIS IDENTITY, SAUL GOODMAN (S'ALL GOOD, MAN) WINDS UP WORKING IN A CINNABON. YOU'D BETTER EAT BUNS WHILE WATCHING *BETTER CALL SAUL* OR YOU'LL LIVE TO REGRET IT – JUST LIKE SAUL LIVES TO REGRET EVER MEETING WALTER WHITE.

200 ml/¾ cup full-fat/whole milk, plus extra to glaze
550 g/4⅓ cups strong white bread flour
60 g/5 tablespoons cold butter, cut into cubes
60 g/5 tablespoons granulated sugar
1 teaspoon salt
7 g/¼ oz. sachet fast-action/rapid-rise yeast
4 egg yolks
1 egg
sunflower oil, for oiling

FILLING
100 g/7 tablespoons unsalted butter, melted
175 g/generous ¾ cup light muscovado sugar
1 tablespoon ground cinnamon
a pinch of salt

ICING
75 g/⅓ cup full-fat cream cheese
3 tablespoons full-fat/whole milk
2 teaspoons pure vanilla extract
150 g/1 generous cup icing/confectioners' sugar

a 20 x 25-cm/8 x 10-inch ovenproof dish, greased

MAKES ABOUT 12

Put the milk in a saucepan set over a gentle heat to warm slightly. Sift the flour into a large mixing bowl and rub in the butter. Stir in the sugar, salt and yeast. Make a well in the middle and pour in the milk, egg yolks and egg. Use a fork to beat the milk and eggs together and start bringing the dry ingredients into the wet until combined. Once the mixture is combined, tip it onto an oiled work surface and knead for 10 minutes, or until the dough is smooth, soft and springy. Put it into a large oiled bowl. Cover with clingfilm/plastic wrap and leave somewhere warm for 1 hour, or until doubled in size.

Knock back/punch down the dough and turn it out onto a work surface. Knead for another minute then roll into a large rectangle about 5 mm/¼ inch thick. Liberally paint this with melted butter, leaving a 2.5-cm/1-inch gap around the edges. Stir together the sugar, cinnamon and salt, and sprinkle it evenly over the dough, then gently press it in.

Beginning with the longest edge of the rectangle facing you, tightly roll the dough into a sausage. Pinch together the seam and roll the sausage over, seam-side down. Cut into 12 equal pieces. Arrange the rolls in the prepared dish, cut-side down and with a little gap in between each one. Cover with a clean kitchen towel and leave somewhere warm for about 1 hour, until doubled in size.

Preheat the oven to 190°C (375°F) Gas 5. Brush the risen dough with milk and bake for 20–25 minutes, until golden and well risen. Mix together the icing ingredients until smooth. Remove the rolls from the oven and leave them to cool slightly before spreading them generously with icing.

"HEY, FOOD IS APOLITICAL."
– TOBY ZIEGLER, *THE WEST WING*

Chapter 8

FEATURED SHOWS
Designated Survivor, Borgen, The West Wing,
Scandal, Homeland, 24.

OTHER SHOWS
Spin City, Madam Secretary, Veep, The Thick of It, Brain Dead,
Alpha House, Commander in Chief, Boss, Spin,
Political Animals, A Very English Scandal,
The Newsroom, Show Me a Hero.

All In A Spin

POLITICS ON A PLATE

WHEN REAL-LIFE POLITICS GETS A BIT MUCH, TUNE IN TO A
POLITICAL DRAMA OR CONSPIRACY THRILLER FOR SOME 'LIGHT
RELIEF' OF CORRUPTION, SCANDAL, DECEPTION, EXTORTION AND
SAGA. WHILE YOU'RE AT IT, WHIP UP SOMETHING IN THE KITCHEN
THAT'S SO TEMPTING EVEN JACK BAUER WOULD TAKE THE TIME TO
PAUSE DURING HIS 24 HOURS FROM HELL TO HAVE A BITE – BEFORE SWIFTLY
RETURNING TO SAVE THE DAY, OF COURSE. THE POLITICAL PROVISIONS
IN THIS CHAPTER ARE THE PERFECT ACCOMPANIMENT TO A NIGHT OF
EDGE-OF-YOUR-SEAT BINGE-WATCHING AS CARRIE MATHISON
WRESTLES WITH HER MENTAL HEALTH AND TERRORISTS, TOM KIRKMAN
REALISES THERE ARE PLENTY OF GREY AREAS IN THE WHITE HOUSE,
OR OLIVIA POPE SLAYS IN A PANTSUIT.

Beef & Mozzarella Sliders
with Pesto Mayo

AS THE OUT-OF-HIS-DEPTH PRESIDENT KIRKMAN AND SENATOR DUNLAP REMINISCE ABOUT THE 'PINESBURGER CHALLENGE' OF THEIR YOUTH IN *DESIGNATED SURVIVOR*, GET YOUR GNASHERS AROUND THESE MINI BURGERS. EAT FOUR AND YOU GET A FREE T-SHIRT.

200 g/7 oz. lean minced/ground beef
2 teaspoons tomato purée/paste
1 garlic clove, finely chopped
4 mozzarella pearls/bocconcini
4 slider buns
a handful of rocket/arugula leaves
sea salt and freshly ground black pepper

PESTO MAYO
200 ml/generous ¾ cup mayonnaise
1 teaspoon fresh green pesto

MAKES 4 SLIDERS

Preheat the oven to 180°C (350°F) Gas 4.

Put the beef in a bowl with the tomato purée/paste, garlic and a pinch of salt and pepper. Work together with your hands until evenly mixed. Divide the beef mixture into quarters and shape into four slider patties. Put a mozzarella pearl in the middle of each and then fold the beef mixture around them to reform the slider patties, with the mozzarella pearl hidden in the middle. Press each slider down to make them nice and flat.

Lay the sliders on a baking sheet and bake in the preheated oven for 20 minutes, turning halfway through cooking. When cooked, remove from the oven and let stand for 4 minutes before serving to allow the mozzarella to cool a little.

Mix together the Pesto Mayo ingredients.

Slice the slider buns in half and spread the bottom half of each with a little Pesto Mayo. Put a cooked slider on top and add a few rocket/arugula leaves. Finish the sliders with the lids of the buns and serve.

Ham & White Asparagus Open Sandwich

OPEN MINDS; OPEN SANDWICHES. WHILE YOU WATCH THE DANISH POLITICAL DRAMA *BORGEN*, WHICH SEES A FEMALE PRIME MINISTER GET ELECTED, ENJOY ONE OF DENMARK'S MOST POPULAR SMØRREBRØD (OPEN SANDWICHES), TOPPED WITH THE PUNCHY 'ITALIAN SALAD'.

butter, for spreading
2 slices of dark seeded rye bread
a small handful of green leaves
4 thick slices of cooked ham
2 white or green asparagus
   spears (see right)
a sprig of chervil or chopped
   chives, to garnish

ITALIAN SALAD
50 g/2 oz. carrots, cooked
   and cubed
50 g/¼ cup frozen peas,
   defrosted
2 tablespoons mayonnaise
2 tablespoons crème fraîche
   or sour cream
tiny bit of Dijon mustard
dash of lemon juice
sea salt and freshly ground
   black pepper

SERVES 2

Traditionally, white asparagus from a jar is used in this topping (you can get these at larger supermarkets/grocery stores), but during asparagus season, you can also use fresh green asparagus. If using fresh green asparagus, you will need to blanch it in boiling water for 2 minutes, then plunge into cold water to stop the cooking process.

Butter the rye bread and arrange it on serving plates. Top the bread with green leaves and arrange the ham on top.

To make the Italian Salad, simply combine all the ingredients together. Season well and arrange on top of the ham with the asparagus. Garnish with chervil or chives and serve.

Egg Cream

ONE SIP OF THIS CHOCOLATEY MILKSHAKE AND YOU'RE SURE TO SHARE THE PRESIDENT FROM *THE WEST WING*'S ENTHUSIASM FOR THE CHILLED BEVERAGE...

BARTLET: TOBY, I'M DRINKING THE MOST FANTASTIC THING I'VE EVER TASTED IN MY LIFE: CHOCOLATE SYRUP, COLD MILK, AND SELTZER. I KNOW IT SOUNDS TERRIBLE, BUT TRUST ME, I DON'T KNOW WHERE THIS HAS BEEN ALL MY LIFE.

TOBY: IT'S CALLED AN EGG CREAM, MR PRESIDENT. WE INVENTED IT IN BROOKLYN.

BARTLET: IN BROOKLYN.

TOBY: YES, SIR.

BARTLET: NOT NEW ENGLAND?

TOBY: THERE ARE SOME GOOD THINGS IN THIS WORLD NOT FROM NEW ENGLAND, SIR.

BARTLET: TOBY, DON'T EVER LET ME HEAR YOU SAY THAT AGAIN.

TOBY: YES, SIR.

2 tablespoons chocolate syrup
250 ml/1 cup milk, chilled
250 ml/1 cup soda water, chilled

2 soda glasses, chilled

SERVES 2

In a jug/pitcher whisk together the chocolate syrup and the milk until all the syrup is dissolved.

Pour the chocolate milk into chilled glasses and top up with the soda. The drinks will foam immediately so you need to serve them straight away.

Red, White & Blue Popcorn

IF THERE'S ONE THING OLIVIA POPE IN *SCANDAL* IS MORE PASSIONATE ABOUT THAN AMERICA, IT'S POPCORN. WHILE SHE'S 'FIXING' POLITICAL SCANDALS, FIX YOURSELF A BOWL OF THIS PATRIOTIC SNACK. IF IT'S TEAMED WITH A GOOD RED WINE, SO MUCH THE BETTER.

1–2 tablespoons sunflower or vegetable oil
90 g/⅓ cup popcorn kernels
80 g/5½ tablespoons butter
red and blue food colouring
60 g/5 tablespoons caster/superfine sugar

MAKES 1 LARGE BOWL

Heat the oil in a large lidded saucepan with a few popcorn kernels in the pan. When you hear the kernels pop, carefully tip in the rest of the kernels. Shake the pan over the heat until the popping stops. Take care when lifting the lid as any unpopped kernels may still pop from the heat of the pan. Divide the popcorn into three bowls, removing any unpopped kernels as you go.

Divide the butter between two small saucepans and heat gently until melted. Add a few drops of red food colouring to one pan and a few drops of blue to the other and stir. Pour the red butter over one of the bowls of popcorn and stir well so that the popcorn is evenly coated. Do the same with the blue butter. The third bowl remains white.

Leave the popcorn to set for about 20 minutes (or the colours will run together). After this time, add all the popcorn to a bowl, sprinkle with the sugar and stir to mix.

Serve in bowls or divide between bags and seal. This popcorn can be served warm or cold, but if you are sealing in bags, make sure the popcorn is cold before you do so.

Baked Moroccan Eggs

PARTLY FILMED IN MOROCCO, *HOMELAND* WILL HAVE YOU ON THE EDGE OF YOUR SEAT. THESE SPICY EGGS ARE MORE EXCITING THAN THE SCRAMBLED EGGS CARRIE ARGUES WITH HER SISTER ABOUT, BUT NOT QUITE AS EXCITING AS HAVING A LOVE AFFAIR WITH A HOMEGROWN TERRORIST.

1½ teaspoons ground cumin
1 tablespoon olive oil
1 onion, cut into thin half moons
1 carrot, grated
1 teaspoon chopped red chilli/
chile
1 red and 1 yellow (bell) pepper,
each cut into 1-cm/½-inch
strips
2 teaspoons salt
2 eggs
2 tablespoons natural/plain
yogurt
1 garlic clove, grated
toasted pita bread, to serve

two 250-ml1-cup ramekins

SERVES 2

Preheat the oven to 180°C (350°F) Gas 4.

Toast the cumin in a dry frying pan/skillet for 30 seconds until it smells nutty. Add the olive oil and onion. Sauté the onion until it is translucent.

Add the grated carrot, chilli/chile and strips of pepper. Sauté for 5 minutes until the peppers have softened their hard edges.

Add 120 ml/½ cup water and turn the heat down to medium. Continue to cook for about 15 minutes until the peppers and onions have relaxed into a gentle compote. You should end up with 250–350 ml/1–1½ cups compote. Season well with salt.

Divide the compote into 2 ramekins, making sure there's at least 2 cm/¾ inch clear at the top of the ramekin. Create a well in the centre of the compote with the back of a spoon. Crack an egg over the top of the peppers. Don't allow the yolk to break.

Float a tablespoon of yogurt over each egg yolk. Sprinkle half a teaspoon of grated garlic over the yogurt. Bake for 16 minutes, until the whites are set, but the yolk is still runny.

Serve with toasted pita bread.

PICKLED CUCUMBER

½ cucumber, washed and thinly
  sliced
3 tablespoons rice vinegar
2 tablespoons caster/granulated
  sugar
1 star anise, bruised

BAO BUNS

500 g/3⅔ cups strong white
  bread flour
2 tablespoons caster/superfine
  sugar
7-g sachet/2 teaspoons
  fast-action yeast
½ teaspoon baking powder
½ teaspoon sea salt
145 ml/scant ⅔ cup lukewarm
  water
145 ml/scant ⅔ cup soy milk
1 tablespoon coconut oil,
  melted
vegetable oil, for greasing and
  brushing

BARBECUED JACKFRUIT

1 x 565-g/20-oz. can green
  jackfruit, drained and rinsed
4–5 garlic cloves, finely
  chopped
1 x 60-g/2-oz. piece of fresh
  ginger, peeled and finely
  chopped
2 tablespoons vegetable oil
2 tablespoons tomato ketchup
5 tablespoons hoisin sauce
2–3 tablespoons caster/
  granulated sugar
2 tablespoons dark soy sauce
2 tablespoons rice vinegar

TO SERVE

1 spring onion/scallion, trimmed
  and thinly sliced at an angle
handful of fresh coriander/
  cilantro
1 tablespoon crushed toasted
  peanuts (optional)

MAKES APPROX. 12–14

Barbecued Jackfruit Bao Buns with Pickled Cucumber

JACK BAUER IS CONSTANTLY FINDING HIMSELF RACING AGAINST THE CLOCK WITH JUST 24 HOURS TO SAVE THE WORLD. WITH ALL THAT RUNNING ABOUT, HIS 'BUNS' ARE SURE TO BE A LOT FIRMER THAN THESE CHINESE STEAMED ROLLS. BUT SOME MIGHT ARGUE, NO LESS YUMMY.

To make the Pickled Cucumber, add all the ingredients to a small bowl and mix well. Set aside.

Mix together all the ingredients for the steamed buns, except the vegetable oil. Knead well using a machine fitted with a dough hook or by hand until it all comes together to make a smooth dough. Place the dough in a well-oiled bowl and cover with clingfilm/plastic wrap. Leave to rest for about 1 hour in a warm place, until doubled in size.

Remove the dough and roll into a giant sausage shape. Divide into approximately 12–14 portions and roll into balls. Using a rolling pin, flatten each ball into an oval. Brush with oil, fold the oval gently in half and place on a well-oiled baking sheet. Rest the buns in a warm place for 30 minutes until risen again.

Prepare the steamer by placing greaseproof paper on the layers and lightly oiling. Put the steamer over a pan of water and bring to the boil. Gently place the buns into the steamer, evenly spaced, and steam for 15–20 minutes. The buns will rise and have a slight bounce when prodded. Set aside.

To make the filling, place all the ingredients in a small pan and bring to a simmer. Cook gently on a low heat for 20–25 minutes until the jackfruit is completely softened. Add a splash of water if the mixture is too dry – it should be soft and sticky-looking. Use a wooden spoon to break up the jackfruit. Fill the buns with a layer of pickled cucumber, a spoonful of jackfruit mixture, spring onion/scallion, coriander/cilantro and a sprinkle of peanuts, if using.

"I LOVE IT HOW YOU'VE SEXUALIZED THE FOOD."
– KENNY POWERS, *EASTBOUND & DOWN*

Chapter 9

FEATURED SHOWS
*Friday Night Lights, Glow, Sports Night,
Arli$$, Eastbound & Down.*

OTHER SHOWS
*30 for 30, The League, Pitch, Blue Mountain State, Hard
Knocks, A Football Life, The White Shadow, SportsCentury,
All American, Ballers, Last Chance U, The Game,
Necessary Roughness, Survivor's Remorse.*

This Sporting Life

TOUCHDOWN TREATS

REMEMBER THAT TIME IN SCHOOL WHEN YOU WON THE GAME IN THE
FINAL SECOND, YOUR TEAMMATES SCOOPED YOU UP, LIFTED YOU ABOVE
THEIR HEADS AND STARTED CHANTING YOUR NAME IN ADORATION WHILE
THE CROWD WENT WILD? NO? OH WELL, NEVER MIND. WITH THESE
SHOWS, YOU CAN RELIVE YOUR SPORTING SUCCESSES – AND FAILURES –
AS YOU NOSH YOUR WAY THROUGH THESE CHAMPION CHOMPS. WHETHER
YOU'RE WHOOPING ALONG WITH MATT'S SUCCESS ON THE FOOTBALL
FIELD IN *Friday Night Lights*, OR WATCHING ZOYA THE DESTROYA
GET A WHOOPING IN THE RING FROM LIBERTY BELLE IN *Glow*, YOU'LL
WANT TO CALL A TIMEOUT (PRESS PAUSE) TO NIP TO THE KITCHEN TO FILL
YOUR PLATE WITH SECONDS. THESE WINNING RECIPES ARE IN A LEAGUE
OF THEIR OWN. IF YOUR GOAL IS TO PARTAKE IN AN EVENING OF GUTS,
GLORY AND GLUTTONY, YOU'RE IN THE RIGHT PLACE. SCORE!

Hot Buffalo Chicken Wing Dip

THROW A 'SUPERBOWL PARTY' WHILE WATCHING THE HIGHS, LOWS AND HUDDLES OF *FRIDAY NIGHT LIGHTS*. THIS FIERY DIP WILL GO DOWN A TREAT AS YOU WATCH COACH TAYLOR INSPIRE HIS TEAM WITH WISE WORDS SUCH AS "CLEAR EYES, FULL HEART, CAN'T LOSE". TOUCHDOWN!

300 g/10½ oz. cream cheese
170 ml/¾ cup ranch salad dressing
125 ml/½ cup red hot chilli/chili sauce (such as Frank's)
150 g/5½ oz. cheddar cheese, grated/shredded
200 g/7 oz. cooked chicken breast
freshly ground black pepper
tortilla chips, to serve

SERVES 6–8

Preheat the oven to 180°C (350°F) Gas 4.

Put the cream cheese, ranch dressing and hot sauce in a bowl and whisk together until smooth. Stir in the grated cheese. Remove any skin from the chicken breasts and discard, then chop into small pieces and stir into the sauce. Season with cracked black pepper and taste. You can add a little salt if you wish, but there should be sufficient salt from the dressing and hot sauce.

Bake in the oven for 25–30 minutes until the top of the dip starts to turn light golden brown. Remove from the heat and leave to cool for a short while then serve warm with tortilla chips.

Variation
Vegetarian buffalo dip: To make a version suitable for vegetarians to enjoy, simply replace the cooked chicken breast with butter/lima beans or small florets of steamed or boiled cauliflower.

Brownie Pops

RESEMBLING LIBERTY BELLE'S WRESTLING COSTUME IN *GLOW*, THESE SWEET BITES WOULD GET THE THUMBS-UP (AND SMACKDOWN) FROM WELFARE QUEEN, WHO SAYS, "SUGAR WAKES ME THE F**K UP. CANDY – CHEAPER THAN DRUGS. TASTES BETTER THAN COFFEE."

200 g/7 oz. dark/bittersweet chocolate, chopped
175 g/1½ sticks butter, diced
250 g/1¼ cups caster/granulated sugar
4 eggs
1 teaspoon pure vanilla extract
125 g/1 cup plain/all-purpose flour
2 tablespoons cocoa powder
75 g/½ cup chocolate chips
3–4 tablespoons apricot jam
½ quantity Chocolate Fudge Frosting; omit the chilli/chile syrup (see page 89)
assorted sprinkles, to decorate

a 20 x 30-cm/8 x 12-inch baking pan, greased and lined
a 5-cm/2-inch round cookie cutter
24 wooden ice lolly/popsicle sticks

MAKES 24

Preheat the oven to 170°C (325°F) Gas 3.

Put the chocolate and butter in a heatproof bowl set over a saucepan of barely simmering water. Stir until smooth and thoroughly combined. Leave to cool slightly. In a separate bowl, whisk the sugar, eggs and vanilla extract with a balloon whisk until pale and thick. Add the melted chocolate mixture and stir until combined. Sift the flour and cocoa powder into the bowl and fold in until well incorporated, then stir in the chocolate chips.

Pour the mixture into the prepared baking pan, spread level and bake on the middle shelf of the preheated oven for 25 minutes. Remove from the oven and leave to cool completely in the pan. (Note: It is easiest to stamp out the brownie rounds if the base is prepared and baked the day before you plan to decorate your brownie pops.)

Remove the cold brownie from the pan. Using the cookie cutter, stamp out 24 rounds from the brownies and arrange on a board or tray. Warm the jam/jelly in a small saucepan, sieve/strain it, then brush it all over the brownie rounds to glaze. Leave on a wire rack for 5–10 minutes to set. Using a palette knife, spread the Chocolate Fudge Frosting evenly all over the rounds, then push a lolly/pop stick into each pop. Lay them on a sheet of baking parchment and leave until the frosting is starting to set. Decorate as desired with an assortment of sprinkles to represent each of the lady wrestlers costumes for fun!

Egg Rolls

JOIN A VERY SLEEPY JEREMY AND A VERY FRAZZLED NATALIE IN THEIR CANDLELIT CHINESE TAKEOUT PICNIC IN *SPORTS NIGHT*. YOU'LL UNDOUBTEDLY LIKE THESE DELECTABLE EGG ROLLS AS MUCH AS JEREMY CONFESSES TO LIKING NATALIE.

3 tablespoons olive oil
1 teaspoon sea salt
1 teaspoon ground black pepper
1 teaspoon ground ginger
1 teaspoon garlic powder
450 g/1 lb. pork shoulder/butt
1 litre/quart groundnut/peanut oil, for frying
2 tablespoons plain/all-purpose flour
120 g/2 cups cabbage, shredded
1 carrot, shredded
8 x 18-cm/7-inch square egg roll wrappers
2 tablespoons sesame seeds (optional)
dipping sauce of your choice, to serve

meat thermometer

MAKES 8

Preheat an oven to 180°C (350°F) Gas 4.

Spread the oil, salt, ground black pepper, ginger and garlic powder on the pork shoulder/butt.

Set the meat on a rack set into a roasting pan. Roast for 20 minutes, and then reduce the heat to 160°C (325°F) Gas 3. Continue to cook until an instant-read thermometer inserted into the shoulder reads 85°C (185°F), about 1–2 hours. Remove the pork from the oven and let stand until cool enough to handle, about 30 minutes. Shred the pork.

Combine the flour with 2 tablespoons water in a bowl until they form a paste. In a separate bowl combine the cabbage, carrots and shredded pork, and mix them together.

Lay out one egg roll wrapper with a corner pointed toward you. Place about 20 g/¼ cup of the cabbage, carrot and shredded pork mixture onto the wrapper and fold the corner up over the mixture. Fold the left and right corners toward the centre and continue to roll. Brush a bit of the flour paste on the final corner to help seal.

In a large frying pan/skillet, heat the groundnut/peanut oil to about 190°C (375°F). Place the egg rolls into the heated oil and fry, turning occasionally, until golden brown. Remove from oil and drain on paper towels or a wire rack. Put on a serving plate and top with sesame seeds if desired.

Serve with a dipping sauce, such as sweet and sour.

Millionaire Jacks

SHOW ME THE MONEY WITH THESE SUPER-RICH 'JACKS. AS YOU WATCH CALLOUS SPORTS AGENT *ARLISS* STATE, "EMOTIONS HAVE NO CASH VALUE", BITE THROUGH THESE LAYERS AND ENJOY THE WEALTH OF CRUMBLY, STICKY, MELTY FLAVOURS.

200 g/7 oz. dark/bittersweet chocolate, broken into pieces

FLAPJACK BASE
150 g/¾ cup light muscovado sugar
150 g/1¼ sticks unsalted butter, softened
2 tablespoons golden/light corn syrup
200 g/1½ cups rolled/old-fashioned porridge oats
a pinch of salt

CARAMEL TOPPING
125 g/1 stick unsalted butter
75 g/⅓ cup light muscovado sugar
25 g/2 tablespoons golden/light corn syrup
1 tablespoon pure vanilla extract
a pinch of salt
1 x 379-g/14-oz. can sweetened condensed milk

a 20-cm/8-inch loose-bottomed square cake pan, greased and lined with non-stick baking paper

MAKES 8 BARS OR 16 SQUARES

Preheat the oven to 150°C (300°F) Gas 2.

For the base, melt together the sugar, butter and golden/corn syrup over a gentle heat, stirring all the time. Take the pan off the heat and stir in the oats and salt until fully combined and coated. Spoon the flapjack mixture into the prepared pan and press it level with the back of a spoon. Bake for 35–40 minutes. Leave to cool in the pan on top of a wire rack.

Meanwhile, make the caramel topping. Place all the ingredients, except the sweetened condensed milk, into a saucepan or pot and stir over a gentle heat until the butter has melted and the sugar has dissolved. Add the condensed milk and increase the heat, stirring frequently, and being careful not to let the base of the mixture catch. Bring to the boil, still stirring every now and then, until the mixture has thickened and turned a deep golden colour. Take the pan off the heat and leave to cool slightly.

Pour the warm caramel over the cooled flapjack base and leave to cool completely.

Place the chocolate in a heatproof bowl suspended over a pan of barely simmering water to melt. Stir every now and then. Once melted, leave to cool slightly before pouring the chocolate over the cold caramel. Leave to cool completely before pushing the base of the pan out and cutting the millionaires' flapjack into 8 bars (alternatively, for smaller portions, you can cut into 16 squares).

Beer-Braised Beef Burrito

THE POTTY-MOUTHED, NON-PC KENNY POWERS IN *EASTBOUND & DOWN* SURE ENJOYS A BEER. IN FACT, HE'S BEEN KNOWN TO DRINK BEER IN THE SHOWER. WHATEVER YOU DO, DON'T FOLLOW HIS EXAMPLE — NO ONE LIKES A SOGGY BURRITO.

400 g/14 oz. braising beef, cut into large chunks
1 large onion, finely chopped
3 garlic cloves, finely chopped
a pinch of ground allspice
1 teaspoon ground cumin
1 teaspoon dried oregano
1 generous teaspoon fine sea salt
250 ml/1 cup beer
400 ml/1½ cups passata/Italian strained tomatoes
2 ancho chillies/chiles in adobo sauce, finely chopped, plus 1 teaspoon of adobo sauce
400-g/14-oz. can black beans, drained
300 g/1½ cups cooked rice
4–6 large flour tortillas
150 g/1½ cups grated/shredded Cheddar or Monterey Jack cheese
freshly ground black pepper
guacamole, to serve

SERVES 4

Combine the beef, onion, garlic, allspice, cumin, oregano, salt and some freshly ground black pepper in a large casserole dish. Add the beer and enough water to cover by about 1 cm/½ inch. Set over a high heat and bring to the boil, then cover and let simmer for 1½–2 hours until the meat is tender.

Strain the meat and transfer it to a chopping board. Return the onion to the casserole dish and reserve 500 ml/2 cups of the broth.

Shred the beef using your hands, or two forks, then return to the pot with the onion. Add the passata/Italian strained tomatoes, ancho chillies/chiles with adobo sauce, beans, 250 ml/1 cup of the reserved broth and the rice. Stir well.

Cook over a medium heat for 15–20 minutes until slightly reduced and thickened. Taste and adjust the seasoning. If the mixture is too thick, add a bit more of the reserved broth, or water.

Preheat the oven to 200°C (400°F) Gas 6.

Divide the beef filling between the tortillas and sprinkle with grated/shredded cheese. Fold in the sides of each tortilla to cover the filling, then roll up to enclose. Place the filled tortillas seam-side down on a greased baking sheet or in a shallow dish.

Cover with foil and bake in the preheated oven for 10–15 minutes just to warm through and melt the cheese. Serve hot with guacamole on the side.

"I'D LIKE A CHEESEBURGER, PLEASE, LARGE FRIES
AND A COSMOPOLITAN."
– CARRIE BRADSHAW, *SEX AND THE CITY*

Chapter 10

FEATURED SHOWS
Sex and the City, The O.C., Desperate Housewives,
Big Little Lies, Gilmore Girls, Girls.

OTHER SHOWS
Dawson's Creek, My So-Called Life, New Girl, Samantha Who?,
Thirtysomething, Party of Five, Gossip Girl, Grace and Frankie,
The Bold Type, One Tree Hill, United States of Tara, Parenthood,
Mom, The Golden Girls, Absolutely Fabulous.

Girls' Night In

SISTA SNACKS

GUYS ARE GREAT AND ALL, BUT THERE'S DEFINITELY SOMETHING WONDERFUL TO BE SAID FOR NOT SHARING THE REMOTE CONTROL ONCE IN A WHILE. MEN JUST DON'T GET WHY CARRIE ET AL FEEL THE NEED TO OVER-ANALYSE WITHIN AN INCH OF THEIR FABULOUS LIVES, WHY GABY IN *Desperate Housewives* FINDS THE GARDENER SO IRRESISTIBLE, OR WHY RYAN IN *The O.C.* IS IN A HABITUAL CYCLE OF 'PUNCH SOMEONE, KISS MARISSA, PUNCH SOMEONE, KISS MARISSA, PUNCH SOMEONE...' BEFORE YOU SLIP INTO YOUR ONESIE AND SNUGGLE UNDER YOUR SOFA BLANKET FOR AN EPIC SESH OF OMG, FOLLOW THE RECIPES IN THIS CHAPTER THAT WILL CURE ANY CRAVING FOR SASSY SUSTENANCE. BRING ON THE CUPCAKES AND COCKTAILS!

Couture Stiletto Cupcakes

FROM CARRIE BEING MUGGED AT GUNPOINT FOR HER MANOLO BLAHNIKS TO GETTING PROPOSED TO BY BIG WITH A SPARKLING STILETTO, SHOES FEATURE SO PROMINENTLY IN *SEX AND THE CITY* THEY SHOULD BE A CHARACTER IN THEIR OWN RIGHT. FORGET THE WALK OF SHAME – IT'S ALL ABOUT THE STRIDE OF PRIDE WITH THESE FABULOUS FASHION STATEMENTS.

200 g/7 oz. white chocolate
12 sweet finger cookies, such as Rich Tea Fingers
edible silver lustre
edible gold glitter spray
12 ready-made plain cupcakes
pink gel or paste food colouring
6 sugar roses
1 tablespoon large edible sugar pearls
12 chocolate wafer rolls

VANILLA BUTTERCREAM
150 g/1¼ sticks butter, softened and cubed
100 g/3½ oz. vegetable fat, such as Trex or Cookeen, at room temperature
1 teaspoon pure vanilla extract
500 g/3½ cups icing/confectioner's sugar, sifted

baking sheet, lined with non-stick baking paper
soft-bristled paintbrush
2 piping/pastry bags fitted with large star nozzles/tips

MAKES 12

Melt 150 g/5 oz. of the white chocolate in a heatproof bowl set over a pan of simmering water. Spread the chocolate over the top of each cookie, leaving 1 cm/½ inch uncovered at the end, allowing the excess to drip back into the bowl. Place the cookies on the prepared baking sheet and put in the fridge to set. Brush with silver lustre and spray with the edible glitter spray.

For the buttercream, whisk together the butter, vegetable fat and vanilla, then slowly beat in the icing/confectioner's sugar.

Divide the buttercream equally between two bowls. Colour one portion pink, leave the second bowl plain. Spread a little of the pink buttercream over the top of six of the cakes. Repeat with the plain buttercream and the remaining six cakes. Spoon the remaining pink buttercream into a piping/pastry bag fitted with the large star nozzle/tip and pipe stars and/or swirls onto six of the cakes. Repeat with the remaining cakes and plain buttercream, using the second piping/pastry bag. Decorate each 'shoe' with cake decorations.

Gently push the uncovered end of the cookies into the buttercream and slightly into the cakes. To create the stiletto heels, melt the remaining 50 g/2 oz. white chocolate as before, cut the wafer rolls at an angle to make sure they sit flush against the biscuit shoes and the work surface, brush with the silver lustre and spray with the gold glitter spray, then attach to the undersides of the cookies using the melted chocolate. Leave to set before wearing (!).

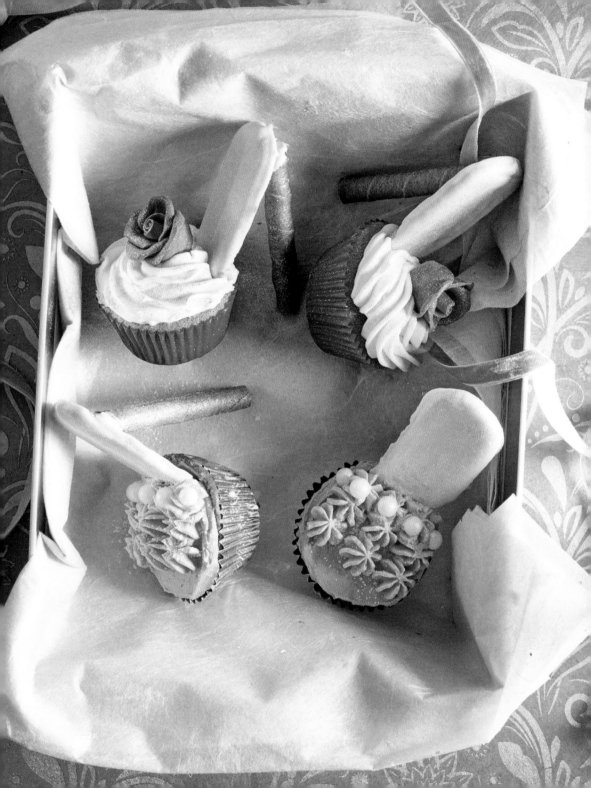

Orange-Marinated Fish Tacos
with Baja Slaw & Chilli Crema

GRAB YOUR SWIMMERS, SUNNIES AND SUNTAN LOTION... IT'S TIME TO GET YOUR CALIFORNIA ON WITH THESE FRESH, FLAVOURFUL TACOS. LIKE *THE O.C.*, THEY'RE HOT, MOREISH AND A LITTLE BIT SAUCY.

juice of 1 orange
2 teaspoons ground cumin
½ teaspoon ancho chilli/chili powder
800 g/1 lb. 12 oz. boneless, skinless white fish fillets (such as tilipia)
8 flour or corn tortillas, warmed
salt
flour, for dusting
vegetable oil, for shallow frying
lime wedges, to serve

BAJA SLAW
4 tablespoons mayonnaise
1 tablespoon lime juice
1 teaspoon salt
a dash of Tabasco sauce
a pinch of ground chumin
1 small white cabbage, thinly sliced
a small bunch of radishes, thinly sliced
a small bunch of fresh coriander/cilantro, finely chopped

CHILLI/CHILI CREMA
6 tablespoons sour cream
2 tablespoons plain yogurt
1 small fresh red chilli/chile, very finely chopped
a small bunch of fresh coriander/cilantro, finely chopped

SERVES 4

To prepare the fish, combine the orange juice, cumin, chilli/chili powder and a pinch of salt in a shallow dish large enough to hold the fish in a single layer. Add the fish and toss well to coat evenly. Cover and leave to marinate in the refrigerator until needed, but preferably overnight. Return to room temperature before cooking.

Mix together the Baja Slaw ingredients and set aside.

To prepare the Chilli/Chile Crema, put the sour cream, yogurt, chilli/chile, coriander/cilantro and a pinch of salt in a bowl. Mix well, cover and set aside until needed.

Remove the fish from the marinade and pat dry with paper towels. Put the flour on a plate, add a pinch of salt and mix well.

Heat 2–3 tablespoons oil in a frying pan/skillet set over a high heat. Dip each fish fillet in the seasoned flour on both sides, shake off the excess and fry for 2–4 minutes on each side, until browned and crisp on the edges and cooked through. Transfer to paper towels to drain.

To serve, arrange a small mound of Baja Slaw in the middle of each tortilla. Top with pieces of the cooked fish and add a spoonful of Chilli/Chile Crema. Serve immediately with lime wedges and extra Chilli/Chile Crema on the side.

Candy Apples

THE OPENING CREDITS OF *DESPERATE HOUSEWIVES* SEE THE INHABITANTS OF WISTERIA LANE CLUTCHING A JUICY, RED APPLE EACH. SINK YOUR TEETH INTO THESE TOFFEE/CANDY APPLES AS STICKY SITUATIONS ABOUND THAT, AS A VOYEUR, ARE JUST TOO TEMPTING FOR WORDS.

4 crisp eating apples
115 g/generous ½ cup caster/
   granulated sugar
25 g/2 tablespoons unsalted
   butter

baking sheet lined with non-stick
   baking paper
4 wooden skewers
a sugar thermometer

MAKES 4

Wash and dry the apples thoroughly.
Push a wooden skewer into the core of each apple nearly the whole way down, but not so that they poke through the other end.

Put the sugar, butter and ½ tablespoon of cold water in a saucepan and heat gently, stirring occasionally. Increase the heat and boil until you reach 132°C (270°F) on a sugar thermometer (soft-crack stage), without stirring.

Take the saucepan off the heat and dip the apples into the toffee mixture one at a time, coating the apples evenly all over. Stand the apples on the prepared baking sheet and leave to set and cool. These are best eaten on the day they are made.

Cucumber Cooler

THE WINE IN *BIG LITTLE LIES* IS FREE-FLOWING. HARDLY SURPRISINGLY, SEEING AS THESE MONTEREY MOMS NEED A DRINK OR THREE TO CALM AND COOL DOWN. MONTEREY IS HOME OF THE CALIFORNIAN ZINFANDEL AND THIS ROSÉ FIZZ WILL HELP YOU DO THE SAME AS YOU'RE SWEPT UP IN ALL THE LIES, VIOLENCE AND INTRIGUE.

1 tablespoon Cucumber Syrup (see below)
about 175 ml/¾ cup sparkling rosé wine, well chilled
a long sliver of cucumber

CUCUMBER SYRUP
225 g/generous 1 cup caster/ granulated sugar
½ cucumber, skin-on and roughly chopped

SERVES 1

First make the Cucumber Syrup. Put the sugar in a small saucepan with 250 ml/1 cup water. Bring to the boil and let simmer for a minute until clear and slightly thickened. Add the chopped cucumber. Leave to cool and transfer to a clean screw-top jar. Refrigerate (for a few hours or overnight if possible) to marinate, then strain the syrup, discard the cucumber pieces, and return the syrup to the jar. The syrup will keep in the fridge for up to 3 weeks.

To make the drink, add the cucumber syrup to the glass and top up with cold sparkling rosé wine. Garnish with a long single sliver of cucumber and serve at once.

Strawberry Pop-Tart Pops

SUGAR MUST RUN THROUGH LORELAI AND RORY'S VEINS IN *GILMORE GIRLS*. THE FIRST TIME LORELAI ATE A POP-TART, IT "TASTED LIKE FREEDOM AND REBELLION AND INDEPENDENCE". JUST LIKE THIS ONE DOES.

240 g/2 cups plain/all-purpose flour, plus extra for dusting
1 tablespoon caster/granulated sugar
1 teaspoon salt
300 g/2¾ sticks butter, diced
1 UK large/US extra-large egg
2 tablespoons very cold milk
1 egg, beaten, mixed with 2 tablespoons milk, for brushing

FILLING
450 g /1 lb. fresh strawberries, hulled and sliced
600 g/3 cups caster/granulated sugar
60 ml/¼ cup freshly squeezed lemon juice
2 tablespoons cornflour/cornstarch mixed with 2 tablespoons water

a crimped pastry wheel
2 baking sheets, greased
24 wooden ice lolly/popsicle sticks

MAKES 20–24

To make the pastry, put the flour, sugar and salt in a food processor and pulse to incorporate. Add the butter and mix on high for 10 seconds until the mixture resembles cornmeal. Beat the egg with the very cold milk and add to the flour and butter mixture. Pulse in the food processor for 20–30 seconds, until the pastry just starts to come together. It should be sticking together, not crumbly. Divide into two balls and wrap with clingfilm/plastic wrap. Chill in the fridge while making the filling.

To make the filling, mash the strawberries in a bowl then put them in a saucepan with the sugar and lemon juice and stir over a low heat until the sugar is dissolved. Increase the heat to high and bring to the boil. Set aside to cool. Once the mixture is cool, set over a low heat, stir in half the cornflour/cornstarch mixture and simmer for 2 minutes. Turn the heat up to high and let boil for 1–3 minutes, just until the jam thickens and coats a spoon. If it isn't thickening, add the second half of the cornflour/cornstarch mixture and boil for 2 minutes more. Remove from the heat and let cool.

Preheat the oven to 180°C (350°F) Gas 4.

Remove the pastry from the fridge. Take one ball and roll it out until 3 mm/⅛ inch thick. (If you want a woven basket-effect finish as shown, roll the pastry out on a lightly-floured piece of textured paper or cloth.) Use a crimped pastry wheel to cut the pastry into 20–24 squares (each 8 cm/3 inches square), then chill in the fridge. Repeat with the remaining pastry. Lay out the pastry squares on greased baking sheets. Brush with egg wash. Put a wooden stick in the middle of half of them and top with 1½ teaspoons of strawberry filling, about 1.5 cm/½ inch from the edges. Place a pastry square on top and seal. Bake in the preheated oven for 15 minutes, or until golden. Take care when serving as the filling will be hot.

Vegetable Dumplings
with Soy Dipping Sauce

HIGH ON POT GUMMIES, LOREEN GORGES ON DUMPLINGS IN A CHINESE RESTAURANT UNTIL HANNAH FINALLY TRACKS HER DOWN IN *GIRLS*. WHEN YOU GET STUCK INTO THESE ONES, LET'S HOPE YOU HAVE LESS TROUBLE WITH YOUR CHOPSTICKS.

1 tablespoon sesame oil
120 g/4 oz. Shitake mushrooms
1 pak choi/bok choy
1 carrot, grated
6 spring onions/scallions, finely
  sliced
2 garlic cloves
1–2 fresh red chillies/chiles
2-cm/¾-inch piece of fresh root
  ginger, grated
a handful of fresh coriander/
  cilantro
1 pack of frozen round dumpling
  (gyoza) wrappers or wonton
  wrappers, defrosted
cornflour/cornstarch, for dusting
sesame oil, for frying (optional)

SOY DIPPING SAUCE
3 tablespoons dark soy sauce
  or tamari
2 teaspoons dark brown sugar
1 tablespoon sesame oil
2 tablespoons rice vinegar (or
  white wine vinegar if you
  don't have it)
1 garlic clove, crushed
1 teaspoon finely grated fresh
  root ginger
½–1 fresh red chilli/chile, very
  finely chopped
a squeeze of fresh lemon juice
a handful of fresh coriander/
  cilantro, chopped

*a bamboo (or other) steamer,
lined with non-stick baking
paper*

MAKES 18

To make the Dipping Sauce, put all of the ingredients in a small bowl and stir until well combined.

To make the dumplings, heat the sesame oil in a frying pan/skillet set over a medium–high heat and add the mushrooms, pak choi/bok choy and carrot. Cook for about 5 minutes, until softened. Put the cooked mushrooms, pak choi/bok choy and carrots in a food processor along with the spring onions/scallions, garlic, chillies/chiles, ginger and coriander/cilantro, and blitz. Alternatively, finely chop all of the ingredients by hand.

Dust the work surface with a little cornflour/cornstarch and put the dumpling wrappers on the floured surface. Put 1 teaspoon of the filling in the centre of each wrapper. Using a pastry brush, moisten the edges of each wrapper with a little water, then seal the edges together. Make sure that the dumpling is well sealed – if not, add a little more water to seal it. You can use your finger to frill the edge of the dumpling for decoration.

Put the bamboo steamer over a pan of boiling water. If you do not have a steamer, cover a colander with a make-shift kitchen foil lid. Put the dumplings in the parchment-lined steamer, cover with a lid and steam for 10–15 minutes until the filling is hot and cooked.

For extra flavour and texture, once the dumplings have been steamed, heat a tablespoon of sesame oil in a frying pan/skillet over a high heat and fry the dumplings for 1–2 minutes, until the bottom and sides start to colour. Be careful as they colour quickly and can easily burn.

The uncooked dumplings will keep covered in the fridge for a few hours. Alternatively, steam the dumplings, let them cool, then store them, well wrapped, in the fridge for a few hours. Re-steam until they are hot again.

"MY BODY IS LIKE A RUM CHOCOLATE SOUFFLE.
IF I DON'T WARM IT UP RIGHT, IT DOESN'T RISE."
– KURT HUMMEL, *GLEE*

Chapter 11

FEATURED SHOWS
*Nashville, Glee, Fame, Flight of the Conchords,
Crazy Ex-Girlfriend.*

OTHER SHOWS
*Star, Victorious, Smash, Pose, The Get Down, Treme,
The Young Ones, Galavant, Behind the Music, Music City,
The Partridge Family, The Monkees, Big Time Rush,
The Singing Detective, Lipstick on Your Collar.*

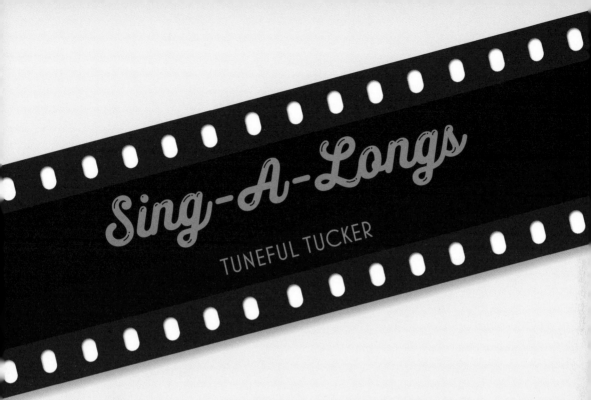

Sing-A-Longs

TUNEFUL TUCKER

SING WHEN YOU'RE WINNING? NAH, SING WHEN YOU'RE EATING! THERE'S NOTHING QUITE LIKE BELTING OUT A SHOW TUNE ALONG WITH YOUR FAVOURITE TV CHARACTER WHILE TRYING TO DIGEST A BREADSTICK. OR BEING TRANSPORTED TO THE BLUEBIRD CAFE AND TAPPING YOUR COWBOY BOOT ALONG TO A TWANG-TASTIC COUNTRY SONG WHILE SHARING THE STAGE WITH YOUR DINING COMPANION, JACK DANIEL'S. FOR YOUR NIGHT OF SING-A-LONG BINGE-WATCHING, YOU NEED TO SING LIKE NOBODY'S LISTENING AND EAT LIKE NOBODY'S JUDGING. THIS ENSEMBLE OF PITCH-PERFECT DELIGHTS WILL HIT ALL THE RIGHT NOTES, SO WHETHER YOU'RE INTO SHOW TUNES, COUNTRY, POP, JAZZ, DISCO, FUNK, ROCK, OR SOMETHING ELSE ENTIRELY, FIND YOUR FOOD OF CHOICE, THEN FIND YOUR VOICE AND SING/EAT YOUR HEART OUT.

Salted Caramel Bourbon & Boozy Chocolate Milkshakes

IT ALL BEGAN FOR TAYLOR SWIFT IN 2004 AT THE BLUEBIRD CAFE, WHICH IS ALSO THE SETTING FOR MANY A COUNTRY SONG BEING BELTED OUT IN *NASHVILLE*. INSTEAD OF 'SHAKING IT OFF', GET YOUR SHAKE ON WITH THESE SPIKED REFRESHMENTS. YEE-HAW!

SALTED CARAMEL BOURBON MILKSHAKE
1 litre/4 cups salted caramel ice cream
250 ml/1 cup chocolate milk
1 teaspoon sea salt
150 ml/⅔ cup bourbon
ice cubes (optional)

SERVES 4

BOOZY CHOCOLATE MILKSHAKE
1 litre/4 cups chocolate ice cream
250 ml/1 cup chocolate milk
1 teaspoon sea salt
150 ml/⅔ cup bourbon
ice cubes (optional)
squirty cream
chocolate flakes

SERVES 2

Salted Caramel Bourbon Milkshake
Blend the ice cream, chocolate milk, sea salt and bourbon in a blender, adding ice depending on how thick you want your shake. Pour into lowball glasses or tumblers.

Boozy Chocolate Milkshake
Replace the salted caramel ice cream with chocolate ice cream and top with squirty cream and chocolate flakes. Makes 2 tall shakes.

Cheesy Grissini

WHILE YOU WATCH THE *GLEE* CREW HANG OUT AT THEIR LOCAL RESTAURANT, BREADSTIX, NIBBLE ON THESE SHOW-STOPPING STICKS DE FROMAGE AND LOOK FORWARD TO THEIR NEXT MUSICAL NUMBER. IT'S SURE TO BE CHEESY AND OH-SO ENTERTAINING.

430 g/3 cups strong white bread flour
7-g/¼-oz. sachet fast-action/ rapid-rise yeast
1 teaspoon fine sea salt
180 ml/¾ cup warm water
1 tablespoon olive oil
3 tablespoons finely grated Parmesan
1–2 tablespoons sesame seeds (optional)

2 or more baking sheets, lined with non-stick baking paper

MAKES ABOUT 24

Sift the flour into a large mixing bowl and stir in the yeast and salt. Make a hole like a well in the middle and pour in three-quarters of the water and all the oil. Stir with a wooden spoon – the dough should be soft but not too sticky.

Add the grated Parmesan to the dough. It will get mixed in when you knead the dough.

To knead the dough, sprinkle a little flour on a clean work surface. Shape the dough into a ball and push on it and press it onto the work surface, turning it round often. You'll need to keep doing this until it is silky smooth and elastic, about 7 minutes.

Shape the dough into a neat ball again. Wash and dry the mixing bowl and sit the dough back in it. Cover tightly with plastic wrap and leave in a warm place until the dough has doubled in size – at least 1 hour.

Preheat the oven to 200°C (400°F) Gas 6.

Tip the dough out onto the floured work surface and knead for 1 minute. Divide it into walnut-sized pieces and roll each piece into a long stick using your hands. Arrange on the prepared baking sheets and let rise again for a further 10 minutes.

Brush some of the grissini with water and sprinkle the sesame seeds over them, if using.

Bake in the preheated oven for 7–8 minutes, or until crisp and golden brown.

New York Cheesecake Bites

LEG WARMERS, LEOTARDS AND FORKS AT THE READY. GET INTO AN EMPIRE STATE OF MIND WITH ONE OF THESE CREAMY CHEESECAKE DELIGHTS. AS YOU TUCK IN, ROOT FOR THE *FAME* WANNABES AS THEY SING AND DANCE THEIR WAY AROUND NEW YORK CITY. BREAK A LEG!

100 g/3½ oz. digestive biscuits/ graham crackers
35 g/2 tablespoons butter, melted
400 g/14 oz. cream cheese
2 UK large/US extra-large eggs
250 g/1 cup sour cream
125 g/⅔ cup (caster) sugar
1 teaspoon cornflour/cornstarch
1 teaspoon pure vanilla extract
finely grated zest and juice of ½ lemon
12 raspberries, plus extra to serve
icing/confectioners' sugar, for dusting

non-stick 12-hole mini cake pan

MAKES 12

Preheat the oven to 170°C (325°F) Gas 3.

Finely crush the digestive biscuits/graham crackers either by blitzing them in a food processor or bashing them in a sealed freezer bag with a rolling pin. Tip the crushed biscuits/crackers into a bowl, add the melted butter and mix until thoroughly combined.

Divide the crumbs evenly between the holes of the cake pan and press down lightly into the base so that they form an even, compact layer. Bake on the middle shelf of the preheated oven for 5 minutes. Remove from the oven but leave the oven on.

Combine the cream cheese, eggs, 100 g/scant ½ cup of the sour cream, 75 g/⅓ cup of the sugar and all the cornflour/cornstarch in a bowl and whisk until smooth. Add the vanilla, lemon zest and juice, and whisk again to combine. Carefully divide the mixture between the holes of the cake pan and push one raspberry into the middle of each cheesecake.

Bake the cheesecakes on the middle shelf of the oven for about 20 minutes or until only just set. Remove from the oven and allow to rest for 5 minutes. Leave the oven on.

Meanwhile, beat together the remaining sour cream and sugar. Carefully spoon this mixture on top of the cheesecakes and return to the oven for a further 5–7 minutes until set but not coloured.

Remove the cheesecakes from the oven and allow to cool completely before refrigerating until chilled.

To serve, carefully push each cheesecake out of the pan and decorate with raspberries. Dust with icing/confectioners' sugar.

Three-Cheese Veggie Lasagne

SING ALONG WITH BRET IN *FLIGHT OF THE CONCHORDS* AS HE BLUBS, "THESE AREN'T TEARS OF SADNESS BECAUSE YOU'RE LEAVING ME... I'VE JUST BEEN CUTTING ONIONS, I'M MAKING A LASAGNE FOR ONE...". ONE TASTE OF THIS LUSCIOUS LASAGNE AND ANY FROWN WILL TURN UPSIDE DOWN.

250-g/9-oz. tub ricotta
180 g/1½ cups chopped frozen
  spinach, defrosted
1 egg
4 tablespoons finely grated
  Parmesan-style vegetarian
  cheese
300-g/10½-oz. package fresh
  lasagne sheets (minimum 8 slices)
90 g/1 cup grated vegetarian
  cheddar
2 x 125-g/4½-oz. balls mozzarella,
  sliced
sea salt and freshly ground
  black pepper

VEGETABLE BOLOGNESE
250 g/2½ cups coarsely chopped
  mushrooms
1 onion, coarsely chopped
1 carrot, coarsely chopped
1 small leek, coarsely chopped
2 garlic cloves
1 celery stick, coarsely chopped
2–3 tablespoons extra-virgin
  olive oil
1 teaspoon dried thyme (optional)
700 ml/2¾ cups passata/Italian
  strained tomatoes
400-g/14-oz. can chopped
  tomatoes
a pinch of sugar
1 dried bay leaf

*a 20 x 25-cm/8 x 10-inch lasagne
  dish or similar baking dish*

MAKES 6–8 SERVINGS

To make the Vegetable Bolognese, put the mushrooms, onion, carrot, leek, garlic and celery in a food processor and process until very finely chopped. Transfer to a frying pan/skillet. Add the oil and thyme, and cook over a medium heat for 3–5 minutes, stirring often, until just beginning to brown. Add the passata/Italian strained tomatoes, canned tomatoes, sugar and bay leaf. Stir to blend, then simmer, uncovered, for at least 15 minutes. Taste and season to taste.

Preheat the oven to 200°C (400°F) Gas 6.

Put the ricotta, spinach, egg, Parmesan-style cheese and a good pinch each of salt and pepper in a mixing bowl and whisk until thoroughly blended.

Spread a thin layer of the vegetable bolognese in the bottom of the lasagne dish and drizzle with a little olive oil. Top with 2 sheets of lasagne. Spread with just under one-third of the bolognese and top with 2 more lasagne sheets. Spread half of the ricotta mixture on top and sprinkle with half the grated cheddar. Top with 2 lasagne sheets then spread with one-third of the remaining bolognese. Top with 2 more lasagne sheets, spread over the remaining ricotta mixture and sprinkle over the remaining cheddar. Top with the remaining lasagne sheets and spread with a good layer of the bolognese.

Arrange the mozzarella slices on top and bake in the preheated oven for 30–40 minutes, until browned and bubbling. Serve hot with a salad.

Chocolate Pretzels

YOU MAY NOT BE ABLE TO HOP ABOARD THESE PRETZELS AND BE HOISTED INTO THE AIR WHILE SINGING ABOUT WEST COVINA, AND THEY'RE PROBABLY NOT GOING TO BURST INTO SONG ABOUT THEIR 'TWISTED FATE', BUT THERE ISN'T A SNACK MORE FITTING FOR A *CRAZY EX-GIRLFRIEND* FEST.

125 g/1 stick butter
250 g/2 cups plain/all-purpose flour
100 g/²⁄₃ cup ground almonds
85 g/scant ½ cup caster/granulated sugar
2 eggs
150 g/5 oz. good-quality dark/bittersweet chocolate, for coating

2 baking sheets lined with baking baking

MAKES ABOUT 25

Preheat the oven to 180°C (350°F) Gas 4.

Rub the butter and flour together in a large mixing bowl until the mixture resembles fine breadcrumbs. Add the ground almonds and sugar. Stir in the eggs and mix until the dough comes together to create a soft dough.

Divide the dough into about 25 small balls and roll each out into very thin sausages. Form each sausage into a pretzel shape by bringing the ends upwards and toward the centre (as if you were forming a circle), cross over the ends, twist and connect each end to the opposite side of the loop. Lift them gently onto the prepared baking sheets, leaving a little room between each.

Bake in the preheated oven for about 10 minutes, until firm and golden. Cool on a wire rack.

Melt the chocolate in a bowl set over a pan of barely simmering water, then dip the pretzels into the melted chocolate to coat. Leave to set on a wire rack. Store in an airtight container in a cool place (but not the fridge), so the chocolate doesn't melt, and eat within 3 days.

Index

Recipe Credits

Brontë Aurell
Ham & White Asparagus
Open Sandwich

Miranda Ballard
Beef & Mozzarella Sliders with
Pesto Mayo

Kiki Bee
Lemon Cake

Mickael Benichou
Coffee Addict's Brownies
Orange Crush Cookies

Julia Charles
Boozy Chocolate Milkshake
Cucumber Cooler

Lydia Clark
Fillet Steak on Toasted
Ciabatta

**Chloe Coker &
Jane Montgomery**
Vegetable Dumplings with
Soy Dipping Sauce

Julian Day
St Clement's Cake

Jesse Estes
Smoking President
Whiskey Sour

**Ben Fordham &
Felipe Fuentes Cruz**
Grilled Shrimp with Green
Salsa
Prawn & Avocado Cocktails

Liz Franklin
Peanut Butter Cookies

Tonia George
Gravadlax with Pickles on Rye
Bread

Victoria Glass
Blue Moon Milkshake
Blueberry Muffins
Cinnamon Buns
Devil's Food Cake
Millionaire Jacks
Pecan Pie
Tawnies

Nicola Graimes
Apple Zinger
Green Giant

Tori Haschka
Baked Moroccan Eggs
Hot Dogs with Remoulade
Sauce
Island Poke
Meatball Deep-Dish Pizza

Carol Hilker
Double-Baked Chicken Wings
Egg Rolls
Fish Finger Sandwich with
Tartare Sauce

Gin Rickey
Pastrami Reuben On Rye with
Russian Dressing
Salted Caramel Bourbon
Milkshake
Spaghetti & Meatballs
Strawberry Pop Tart Pops
The Bee's Knees

Jennifer Joyce
Mama's Meatloaf

Jackie Kearney
Barbecued Jackfruit Bao Buns
with Pickled Cucumber

Dan May
Mini Crab Cakes with Chilli
Lime Mayo

**Claire McDonald &
Lucy McDonald**
Cherry Pavlova

Hannah Miles
Bloody Mary Granitas
Egg Cream
Hot Buffalo Chicken Wing Dip
Peanut Waffles with Snickers
Ice Cream
Ranch Dip with Sweet Potato
Chips
Red, White & Blue Popcorn
Scottish Oatcakes
Strawberry Shortcake Sundae
Sunflower Seed Popcorn
Trifle Cheesecakes

Suzy Pelta
Garbage Cookies

Annie Rigg
Brownie Pops
Cheesey Grissini
New York Cheesecake Bites

Angela Romeo
Couture Stiletto Cupcakes

Tristan Stephenson
Blood & Sand

Milli Taylor
Empanadillas

Nicki Trench
Candy Apples

Lily Vanilli
Meringue Bones with Cherry
Sauce
Zombie Hands Cupcakes

Laura Washburn
Beer-Braised Beef Burrito
Matchstick Fries with Sichuan
Pepper Salt
Orange-Marinated Fish Tacos
with Baja Slaw & Chilli
Crema
Three-Cheese Veggie Lasagne

Picture Credits

Food photography:

Martin Brigdale 50; **Peter Cassidy** 5ac, 23, 49, 59, 63, 74, 77, 110, 127, 149; **Helen Cathcart** 56; **Jean Cazals** 27; **Addie Chinn** 41; **Laura Edwards** 124; **Tara Fisher** 19, 114; **Jonathan Gregson** 60; **Winfried Heinze** 139; **Mowie Kay** 46, 123; **Adrian Lawrence** 78, 135; **Lisa Linder** 150; **William Lingwood** 11; **Alex Luck** 32, 42, 97, 102, 140; **David Munns** 28, 35; **Steve Painter** 2, 20, 64, 69, 70, 73, 83, 143; **William Reavell** 12, 144; **Toby Scott** 1, 55; **Stuart West** 101; **Kate Whitaker** 5bc, 31, 91, 92, 113, 153, 154, 157; **Isobel Wield** 5b, 16, 36, 84, 87, 88, 98, 105, 117, 131, 136; **Clare Winfield** 15, 109, 118, 128.

TV stills:

6l AF archiv/Alamy Stock Photo; 6r Erica Parise/©Netflix/courtesy Everett Collection/Alamy Stock Photo; 7l Greg Gayne/© The CW Network/courtesy Everett Collection/Alamy Stock Photo; 7ar & br Photo 12/Alamy Stock Photo; 10 AF archive/Alamy Stock Photo; 13 Everett Collection Inc/Alamy Stock Photo; 14 TCD/Prod.DB/Alamy Stock Photo; 17 Photo 12/Alamy Stock Photo; 18 Pictorial Press Ltd/Alamy Stock Photo; 21-22 PictureLux/The Hollywood Archive/Alamy Stock Photo; 26 AF archive/Alamy Stock Photo; 29 PictureLux/The Hollywood Archive/Alamy Stock Photo; 30 © BBC-America/Courtesy: Everett Collection/Alamy Stock Photo; 33 AF archive/Alamy Stock Photo; 34 PictureLux /The Hollywood Archive/Alamy Stock Photo; 37 AF archive/Alamy Stock Photo; 40 WENN Rights Ltd/Alamy Stock Photo; 43 Photo 12/Alamy Stock Photo; 44 Everett Collection Inc/Alamy Stock Photo; 47 Moviestore collection Ltd/Alamy Stock Photo; 48 AF archive/Alamy Stock Photo; 51 Craig Blankenhorn/©FX/courtesy Everett Collection; 54 Photo 12/Alamy Stock Photo; 57 Everett Collection Inc/Alamy Stock Photo; 58 Moviestore collection Ltd/Alamy Stock Photo; 61 Everett Collection Inc/Alamy Stock Photo; 62 © Globe Photos/ZUMAPRESS.com/Alamy Stock Photo; 65 PictureLux/The Hollywood Archive/Alamy Stock Photo; 68 Everett Collection Inc/Alamy Stock Photo; 71 Paul Drinkwater/NBC/NBCU Photo Bank via Getty Images; 72 Moviestore collection Ltd/Alamy Stock Photo; 75 ©Amazon/Everett CollectionMoviestore collection Ltd/Alamy Stock Photo; 76 Ron Batzdorff/NBC/NBCU Photo Bank via Getty Images; 79 AF archive/Alamy Stock Photo; 82 Photo 12/Alamy Stock Photo; 85 & 86 Photo 12/Alamy Stock Photo; 89 Everett Collection Inc/Alamy Stock Photo; 90 © Warner Bros. Television/Courtesy Everett Collection Alamy Stock Photo; 93 Allstar Picture Library/Alamy Stock Photo; 96 AF archive/Alamy Stock Photo; 99 AF archive/Alamy Stock Photo; 100 Everett Collection Inc/Alamy Stock Photo; 103 & 104 AF archive/Alamy Stock Photo; 108 Sven Frenzel/Getty Images; 111 & 112 Photo 12/Alamy Stock Photo; 115 AF archive/Alamy Stock Photo; 116 Moviestore collection Ltd/Alamy Stock Photo; 119 Pictorial Press Ltd/Alamy Stock Photo; 122 & 125 Everett Collection Inc/Alamy Stock Photo; 126 & 129 PictureLux/The Hollywood Archive/Alamy Stock Photo; 130 AF archive/Alamy Stock Photo; 134 HBO/Newsmakers/Getty Images; 137 Everett Collection Inc/Alamy Stock Photo; 138 Allstar Picture Library/Alamy Stock Photo; 141 Pictorial Press Ltd/Alamy Stock Photo; 142 PictureLux/The Hollywood Archive/Alamy Stock Photo; 145 Photo 12/Alamy Stock Photo; 148 Katherine Bomboy-Thornton/ABC via Getty images; 151 Photo 12/Alamy Stock Photo; 152 Everett Collection Inc/Alamy Stock Photo; 155 Allstar Picture Library/Alamy Stock Photo; 156 Everett Collection Inc/Alamy Stock Photo.